The Foxes' Union

The Foxes' Union

And Other Stretchers, Tall Tales,
And Discursive Reminiscences of Happy Years
in Scrabble, Virginia

James Jackson Kilpatrick

EPM Publications, Inc.
McLean, Virginia

Library of Congress Cataloging in Publication Data

Kilpatrick, James Jackson, 1920-
    The foxes' union.

    I. Title.
AC8.K482   081   77-23340
ISBN 0-914440-18-7
ISBN 0-914440-63-2 pbk

Design by Charles O. Hyman

DATELINE: SCRABBLE

I began writing my syndicated column, "A Conservative View," in the summer of 1964. For the next two years I ground away at conventional grist: Politics, government, and law. But on a November day in 1966, thinking a change of pace might be welcome, I wrote a little country piece under the dateline of Scrabble, Virginia.

The dateline was a stretcher to start with. Our post office actually is at Woodville. Scrabble is a community two miles on down the road toward Culpeper. But what writer with an ounce of poetry in his veins would choose *Woodville* as a dateline, when with a spark of honest larceny he could latch onto *Scrabble* instead?

Scrabble it was. Over the next ten years I wrote a hundred such columns. They provoked an astonishing and gratifying response. Evidently thousands of city dwellers, growing up in an urban environment, retain some umbilical tie to the land; readers in rural areas were pleased to find a kindred spirit in a columnist far away. Gradually an idea took root that maybe the Scrabble pieces would add up to a book.

It proved impossible simply to clip and paste an anthology together — impossible for me, anyhow. Except for a few columns that have been folded in verbatim, this little book is written mostly from scratch. Part I is largely personal stuff, dealing with White Walnut Hill and our life there. Part II has to do with Rappahannock County and the Rappahannockers. Part III includes some observations on birds and animals, among them members of Local 211, the Foxes' Union. Part IV covers the black-eyed pea and other botanical glories. Part V is a lumping together of reflections that didn't fit anywhere else.

In the decade embraced by these reminiscences, I wrote perhaps 2.5 million words of sober stuff—columns, speeches, TV commentaries, magazine articles, thousands of letters. Nothing provided nearly as much personal pleasure as the copy that carried my dateline: Scrabble.

James Jackson Kilpatrick

White Walnut Hill
May, 1977

Part One

In answer to the newspaperman's
Who, What, Where, When and Why.

On a Saturday in late January, 1966, Marie and I drove up to Washington from Richmond. I had been lassoed for a black tie dinner, and she wanted to catch a White Sale at Woodie's. We holed up at the old Congressional Hotel, which was then my home away from home, and Sunday morning after breakfast, with the papers in a terminal moraine across the room, she turned to the classified section of the *Star* while I studied my favorite intellectual section of the *Post*. As I absorbed Prince Valiant, she scanned the ads on mountain property.

"This one sounds interesting," she said.

It was hard to get my attention. This was the morning after Alfalfa Club the night before, and Prince Valiant demanded exceptional concentration. Besides, Dick Tracy was in deep trouble and the young lovers in Mary Worth had parted in anger. Rex Morgan's patient was dying. It was a typically tragic morning in the funnies.

"Hmmm," I said.

Marie persisted. "Listen," she said. And she read it aloud:

RAPPAHANNOCK COUNTY — 36 ac., good view mtns, mostly clear, four-room cottage. 675-3691.

"Hmmm," I remarked. I was into Moon Mullins, thinking deeply.

We had been married for 23 years. A wife learns *something* about her husband in 23 years. She came over and kissed me behind the right ear. She had my attention. "Look," she said, "you can at least call."

I got up, and stretched, and looked out the window onto Capitol Hill. Washington is the seat of the greatest free government on earth, but on a cold Sunday morning in January it fails to inspire. It had been snowing for three days, and the sky was the color of old sweat shirts. The streets were glazed. Scoops of lumpy snow were mounded at the curbs like leftover potatoes on a greasy platter. I thought of reasons not to drive out to a place in Rappahannock County.

"It's probably knee-deep in snow," I said. "If we got stuck

we'd never get back to Richmond." She kissed me behind the other ear. I reached for the phone.

We had been looking—actually *she* had been looking—for a place in the mountains for a couple of years. A year or so earlier, while I was still editor of the Richmond *News Leader*, I had started writing a syndicated column for *Newsday*, which wanted one conservative to balance its six liberal pundits. In August of 1965, I had switched over to the Washington *Star.*

The column had gone well. Little by little it became inevitable that I would leave Richmond for a new base of operations in Washington, but it was a big leap. We kept hesitating. I was a happy clam in the drowsy sands of Richmond. No editor could have asked for more — freedom to write, a competent staff, congenial associates, a superlative publisher upstairs, good hot metal printers in the composing room. Ambition called; procrastination answered. Meanwhile, a seed of an idea had begun to germinate in my wife's mind: Wouldn't it be nice, she kept saying, to have a little weekend place in the mountains, not too far from Richmond, not too far from Washington? She was forever looking at road maps and circling classified ads.

Newbill Miller answered the telephone. He seemed oddly cautious about showing the 36-acre place. There was a good deal of interrogatory conversation about who I was, and what we were looking for. The farm, he said, was badly run down. It would take a lot of work to clean it up. He was being an unsalesman. It wasn't until much later that we came to understand that being admitted to Rappahannock County was like making the Cosmos Club. This sense of possessive exclusivity persists. The true Rappahannocker believes his county is just about perfect as it is, and he perceives no convincing reason to risk the admission of a stranger. Besides, said Newbill Miller, the roads were knee-deep in snow.

We gave up, and drove home to Richmond. I didn't really want to think about a place in the mountains anyhow, for we had other pressing concerns. One son was having academic disasters, another son was mending a broken heart, and still another son was about to join the Marines. Anyone who has three sons will understand.

Two weeks passed before these upheavals subsided, and it wasn't until February 6 that we drove up to Washington, Virginia, to meet Newbill Miller at the County Courthouse. I pause to explain that in the common parlance of newcomers to our county, Washington, Virginia, is known as little Washington, the better to distinguish it from the other Washington 80 miles away. The appellation is locally regarded as offensive. The town that forms our county seat existed long before the capital of the nation came into being, and Rappahannockers are great believers in the seniority system. The correct usage, if a Rappahannocker has motored into Washington, D.C., is to say that he is spending the day in the District. Standing alone, "Washington" means Washington, Virginia, population 189, and that was where we met Newbill Miller.

It was one of those superbly beautiful days that Virginia provides in the midst of winter drearies. The whole morning had been washed and the clouds hung out between the mountains to dry. Rappahannock's rolling meadows were still deep in an unsmudged snow, but the winding roads were clear. We bundled into his station wagon and he plunged the car off the main highway, across the Thornton River, down a hollow, and up a hill.

"That's it," said Newbill Miller. He sounded as if it wasn't much. "It's known as the June Corbin place."

The truth is, it wasn't much. Snow had drifted ten feet high, so there was no way of getting up to the empty cottage. Here and there, the wind had blown the fields into patches of bare brown skin. These bore an unkempt beard of broom sedge. We could see a swaybacked barn, a roofless chicken house, a capacious privy. At the bottom of the hill, close by the road, a shack perched on stilts beside a crumpled pigpen. In the brilliant stillness, the place breathed slowly of abandonment.

But there was more than abandonment. The cottage had a sturdy look. It stood in a grove of towering oaks and maples.

Out front were some fine old boxwoods: signs of love. As far as we could see, to the north and east and west, snowy meadows rippled to the dark and slumbering mountains. We lifted our eyes to the hills. Then, as suddenly as a skyrocket, a pileated woodpecker soared from the woods, splashing scarlet pigment on a landscape done in brown and white. The pileated is the largest and handsomest of our surviving woodpeckers. For fifteen years, since we first had seen one in the Allegheny Mountains, the pileated woodpecker had been a bird of special meaning to us: a bird of love. We looked at each other, and nodded. And that was how we bought the June Corbin place.

Newbill Miller unfolded a map. We were two miles from Woodville, off Route 522; we were four miles from Scrabble, six miles from Sperryville, eight miles from Washington, and 17 miles from Culpeper. We were, in brief, pretty well out in the boonies.

We looked at a plat. The 36 acres of the Corbin place formed a long thin crescent on the west side of a graveled, roller-coastery country road, known to natives as the Rudasill's Mill Road, and to the State as Route 621. The property was bounded on the south by White Walnut Run, on the north by the pigpen and a spring-fed creek. To the west, a sentinel line of bare trees stood at ease along the meadows of Mr. Burke. To the east, a surf of small hills broke on the slopes of Red Oak Mountain.

It was love at first sight. Newbill Miller, who knows when he has a customer hooked, folded up the map, gave us an extra plat to play with, and drove us back to the Courthouse.

Two weeks later we came back to close the deal. The snow had melted. What had been pure beauty was now pure mud. Newbill Miller was there waiting for us. In a few minutes June Corbin rattled up in an old black pickup truck. He dismounted with the stiffness of age and trudged over to extend a gnarled hand, blue-veined, thin as a leaf. He seemed very old and very frail. He had dressed for the formal occasion in an immaculate white shirt, but the shirt must have fit him in a better time. Now it hung slack around his wattled neck.

11

Newbill Miller put one foot on the front bumper of his station wagon, and spread some papers on the hood. He began to read aloud the deed of bargain and sale, pausing after every sentence to ask, "Do you understand, Mr. Corbin?" At first the old gentleman said, "yes, yes," but in a few minutes his eyes filled with tears and he only nodded mutely. We looked away, embarrassed.

God knows it must have been hard for June Corbin to part with the place. He had built the cottage himself in the mid-twenties, out of oak logs he felled and sawed into siding on the site. The stumps are still there today, as big around as barrels. June and his wife Mae raised five children in the four-room cottage, with nothing but a cold-water sink, a potbellied stove, and a four-hole privy. Late in life, as we heard the story, they had a falling out. Mae stayed in the cottage on top of the hill; June built himself a shack by the pigpen below. When communication could not be avoided, they hollered up and down the hill. Now, in 1966, their children were grown and married. The outbuildings were falling to pieces. It was time to sell.

Newbill Miller finished his reading. We all signed papers, holding them down against a fine March wind, and after a while we were left alone to inspect what we knew, even then, would turn out to be our last, best, and most-loved home: White Walnut Hill.

Let me say a word about the eye of the artist, more precisely about the eye of a sculptor. It is not like the eye of a newspaperman. The reporter tends to see what is, the sculptor what can be. Marie is a sculptor. She looks upon a walnut log or a great chunk of marble, and sees the form within. All that remains is to carve away the excess, and behold: The form was there all along. Thus Marie looked upon the cottage, the rickety hen house, the four-hole privy, the spavined barn, and the scraggly fields, and found them good. We sat on the worn floor and drew plans.

By the end of March the plumber Quinn had arrived, a

stage Irishman, stooped from the crawl spaces he had known. Electricians came and went. One day a giant bulldozer rumbled into action, dug a tremendous hole, pushed the barn, the privy, and the hen house into the hole, covered the rotting mess with dirt, and rumbled away. In the rich earth down by the pigpen, Marie planted neat rows of peas and lettuce. The place was coming along.

It became apparent that, while the specialists were fine, what we needed was an expert. We found him in Charlie Settle, who was long-limbed and long-armed and built like a whooping crane. His formal education was nil, or next to it, but he knew a thousand things you cannot find in books. By happy circumstance, in the University of Nature he had taken his Ph.D. in springs.

That was what we needed most urgently: a spring doctor. The Corbins had relied for a water supply on a spring at the foot of the hill, maybe 50 yards upstream from the pigpen. For lack of use the spring had turned into a muddy bog. Before we got onto Charlie, a sanitary engineer from the health department, possessed of an honest-to-VPI degree, came and inspected the possibilities, turned up his nose, and suggested we drill a deep well instead. A second consultant, equally learned in hydraulic theory, sketched an elaborate array of cylindrical cisterns. What we wanted was a simple spring box, a pump, and a pipeline. Charlie knew what we wanted.

A city boy has no real measure of his ignorance until he undertakes to fathom the workings of a spring. You have to have a sixth sense of how water moves, deep in the earth; how water finds a spring rock, and how it lies under the spring rock; and then you have to know — carefully, carefully! — just how to free the water from the stone, guide it to a reservoir, and bring it to a pump. Charlie knew these things. He waded into the mud, shin-deep. His shovel became a magic wand. He gazed with a pure intensity at the slow trickle that became a steady stream, thick as your wrist. Then the water leaped up, lithe as a snake, free of the mud and muck. "Theah she is," said Charlie, "theah she is."

We had a water system, courtesy of Charlie Settle. We had electric power, courtesy of the Northern Piedmont Co-op. We had a one-hole john and a shower, courtesy of Mr. Quinn. We had a working kitchen. two usable bedrooms, a living room with a Franklin stove. We were in business, coming up from Richmond on weekends, and there was time for the drawing of long breaths.

Spring came late to Scrabble that first year. It wasn't until April 12, I noted in my journal, that my spading fork turned up the earth smell. The scent rose from the red Rappahannock dirt as unmistakably as the smell of open fires in fall: a warm smell, warm as bread, pregnant as the swelling buds, the smell of spring at last.

It had been a long winter for old-time Rappahannockers— long, and nothing really to be said for it. With one exception the snows were ordinary, average snows, sort of used-car snows, not bad, but not exciting either. They were not the kind of snows you mark a birth or death by. The worst of it was that the snow kept hanging around; it wore its welcome out; you could not make it go home. It lingered in shady spots; it slept under the eaves like old dalmatians.

Ordinarily Virginia succors her country people with a truly warm spell in February, with a few days of temperatures in the 70's, enough to melt the snow clean away. This year was an exception. While we fretted in impatience, the ground stayed frozen for weeks on end. Morning fogs hung on the hills like dirty curtains. Nothing stirred. The Black Angus cattle were somnolent black shadows in the dun, indifferent fields. Men stayed at home and puttered. Ned Johnson built some wren houses. A couple of aging gentlemen, silent as stones, sat around the stove at the Woodville Post Office. It was our first experience with the Waiting Time.

Late in March a nine-year-old boy came up from Richmond with his mother, to spend his first day in the country. It had been too cold for flying kites, but this particular morning had the kite feel. It was the only thing to do with so crisp a morning, to fly a kite in it. We walked to the high meadow, tearing an old pink and yellow pillowcase in strips to make a tail.

Do you remember what it is to fly a kite with a boy? The boy runs with the kite—a kite with a clown's face—and a breeze lifts it gently, tentatively, uncertainly, into the air. The moment is a moment of pure suspense: Orville on the beach at Kitty Hawk. The kite climbs up the sky—up, and up—and staggers for an instant, then up again, finds its element; and flies.

So it was that morning. We sat for half an hour on a moss green rock, seldom speaking. The kite tugged at the line like some great fish, hooked to the earthbound angler; the kite swam in the invisible currents of the wind, pulling and darting. Then the boy hauled the kite in, and ran to where it fell, and returned clutching his clown-trophy. He had never flown a kite before.

From the high meadow we could see White Walnut Run, swollen from bank to bank, the rapids tumbling like puppies. The willows were pale jade fountains by the bridge. Where does the stream go, asked the boy? To the Thornton River, I said. Pause. And where does the Thornton go? To the Rappahannock. And where then? To the Chesapeake Bay, I said, but it was a feeble lesson in geography. I might better have said, to the distant sea, to the sea where galleons once sailed under canvas clouds, to the blue-green sea where crabs crawl and dolphins dance, and mermaids play by foamy cliffs. At nine, a boy ought to hear these things.

This was a spring of discovery. Every spring, of course, is a spring of discovery, but first discoveries are the sweetest. We looked into the fairy chalice of a dogwood bud, the seeds of summer clustered in a sturdy cup. We explored the narrow country roads, discovering the wild flowers. On the road that hugs the dark breast of Bessie Bell Mountain we found bloodroot and hepatica, white and blue and pure gold inside. We found columbine, wild iris, bird's-foot violets, tiny ferns as perfectly louvered as the shutters on a doll's house.

When the earth smell finally became perceptible, and the land yawned and rubbed its eyes, we went to the top of Red

Oak Mountain. It is not as high as Old Rag or Hawk's Bill, of course, but it is the highest point for miles around. It was like going to the top of the world. Two or three weeks earlier we would have seen little but sepia fields and dark olive mountains. Now a miracle had passed our way. The fields were washed in lavender and green, the apples dressed in ruffled lace, the land alive again.

These were moments of mute surprise. What a discovery it must have been, unnumbered eons past, when brute man first grasped the meaning of the seasons! What passed through his primitive mind in autumn? The leaves fell and plants died, and his world turned to darkness and to winter's death. Was his world ending?

Perhaps this blinking troglodyte, walking upon a mountainside in spring, thought of the gods he feared and worshipped; They had not deserted him. *Look!* The bud opens, the leaf uncurls; the earth was not dead, but only sleeping. Perhaps he too thrust his clumsy fingers into April, pushing aside the rotted leaves, and humble on his knees beheld the bursting seed. It was his mystery then; and it is ours now.

The spring of '66 moved on to summer. Marie set to work with Charlie Settle, down the hill where the pigpen used to be, to convert Mr. Corbin's little shack into a sculptor's studio. Again, it was a matter of the artist's eye and the artisan's hand. I myself looked at the shack and saw only a 12 x 12 shack, hanging like a bird's nest to the hillside. You had to climb 14 feet of outside steps to reach the door. I looked at the hillside and saw only a jungle of honeysuckle, briars and poison ivy.

Marie looked at the shack and said: Here I will have a small room for painting when I feel like painting. And here, where the steps are, I will attach a high beamed room for sculpturing, with a fireplace on the west wall and windows all around. Here I will keep my clay wet, and here I will store logs for seasoning, and here, where the hogs once wallowed, I will work on wood and stone. Above the shack we will build a stone wall to keep the hillside in its place. We will have rhododendrons, azaleas, and laurel, and ferns. Charlie scratched his stubbled cheek, and pulled on his ear, and said, yes, ma'am. So they built it.

I worked on other chores, and our sons worked, and we watered the stubborn grass with our sweat, but it wasn't all work. One day in June we drove over to a kennel in Culpeper County, and knelt beside a fenced-in run where collie puppies were playing. There we were adopted by a tricolored bundle of pure joy, black and brown and white, and this was to be Lorenzo de Medici of White Walnut Hill, a very long name for a very small puppy. We had owned half a dozen dogs before — a beagle, a black cocker, a beloved dachshund — but never a dog like Lorenzo. In another six weeks he grew to match the size of his feet, and we thought he would never stop growing thereafter.

We found time, that summer, simply to lean on a split-rail fence, to study the architecture of a robin's nest, to revel in the burnt-orange brilliance of day lilies by the road. From the back porch of the cottage we could watch the Burkes make hay — father, son, and son-in-law, toiling all day long. Looking on, I wondered what riches we city folk may claim, one-half so precious as the hard but yielding land that holds the countryman's devotion.

God's handiwork lies in cities, too, in books and bridges and in buildings, and the city can be loved and hated just as deeply as the soil. Yet to cultivate a love for one's own land, as another Burke reflected years ago, is to forge the first link in the chain that leads from a love of one's own community to a love of country, and thence to a love of all mankind.

The honeysuckle, sweet-perfumed, grows in profusion every June. It tumbles like a woman's windblown ringlets upon the shoulders of our country lanes, russet-stemmed, dark-leaved, and some of it is red and some is gold. In time it cloys; it gets to be a nuisance. You cannot get rid of the stuff. It is the love that smothers in its own choking embrace. I pass the metaphor along to any novelist who may put it to good use: Honeysuckle is beautiful; and it is hateful also.

If the honeysuckle can be loved somewhat, the briars cannot be loved at all. Nor the poison ivy. Nor the trumpet vine. Nor the rocks that nick the mower blades. Down in Richmond, the computer programmers of the Motor Vehicles Division worked out code names for the counties of Virginia. They took the first letter and the last three, so that Arlington came out ATON, and Fairfax FFAX, and Henrico HICO. Rappahannock County, naturally, came out of the computer as ROCK, which is mostly what our county is. Rockyhannock, the land we love.

And it *is* a land to be loved. That first summer of discovery, we learned the delight that flows from ordinary things — a square dance of daisies, dressed in white and gold, doing allemande rights and allemande lefts, and do-si-dos in the wind. We found images of jewelry — buttercups by Cellini, strawberry tiaras, clover ruby-red.

One thinks of rural living in terms of "the quiet of the country," but the country is not quiet. Late of a June afternoon one listens. Far away a tractor strains; the hay rake clatters and the baler thumps and grunts, a peristaltic beast that slouches its clumsy way across the hills, leaving his heavy spoor behind. The Burkes are in their highest meadow now, working the ruffled windrows; they are half a mile away, at least, but the mountains have a trick with sound. The parabolic slopes pick up the voices of the men, calling back and forth.

Men and machines are universally familiar sounds. One listens. There is a bass viol section playing pianissimo, bay-windowed bumblebees, black-tied; wasps, crickets, softly swarming things — they saw away like second violins. But rising constantly above their muted murmuration, like the sound of horns from unseen city streets, there comes the conversation of the birds.

They are in a gabby mood this afternoon, these Rappahannock County birds — cardinals, jays, robins, two busy wrens, a dowager oriole trailing rose chiffon. Up in the orchard a crow is cawing as persistently as some old congressman, rasping his objections to an inattentive House. The quail blow their bobwhite whistles. These birds might as well be playing bridge, chattering away at the play of a good hand.

Toward the end of 1966 I resigned my post in Richmond, moved Marie into the cottage full-time, and bought a little house at 905 G Street, S.E., within walking distance of the Capitol. I worked in Washington, learning my new beat; she worked in her studio in Rappahannock. Five days a week we were 80 miles apart. It was not good. I fell in with a low companion, a yellow alley cat by the name of John L. Sullivan. He was a freeloading old pug who had licked every cat in the Navy Yard and boasted incessantly of his triumphs. Sullivan was a great talker, but he got to be a bore. After a while my oldest son Sean took a job in Washington and moved in with me. That helped, but Marie was still alone in the country — and, well, it was not good.

So in the late spring of 1967 we began to plan all over again. Just to the west of the cottage is a towering chestnut oak, dominating a white walnut, a gnarled old gum, a persimmon, a couple of aging dogwoods. It seemed a spectacular building site. From the beginning she saw the home we would build there.

"Here," she said, digging a small heel in the scrubby ground, "will be the corner of the living room. And here," pointing to the north, "will be glass doors looking out to the high meadow and to the mountains."

I easily caught the contagion. "Here," pounding on a stake with a stone, "will be a little working office area off a bedroom, where I can look at Old Rag to the west."

"We will bring in a new driveway," she said, "that will curve into the glory of Red Oak Mountain in October."

"There will be great stone fireplaces," I said, "and we will stack the firewood here."

19

We drove a hundred stakes after that, and Lorenzo pulled up most of them because that is the way collies are. They are incorrigible practical jokers. We measured, and we made notes, and we drew sketches, and we watched the way the shadows fell. We squabbled over which way dream doors would open. Floyd Johnson, our architect, came and went, and puffed on his pipe, and returned with rolls of drawings. At Christmas, we exchanged presents that would go in the someday house. It was never out of mind.

"What do you think of George Romney's chances?" I would ask. This was before New Hampshire, in early 1968.

"I wonder if we've planned enough bookshelves," she would say.

So the winter passed, and another spring and summer, and the Chicago convention, and 1968 rolled on to October. I was in Portland with Nixon or in Wilkes-Barre with Muskie. One forgets. The backs of all press buses look the same. A telephone rang in a hotel room.

"Guess what," she said. Her excitement spanned the miles. "They've started on the foundations."

That was as far as we got before the snows of November set in. All winter long, our knoll looked like the ruins of Pompeii, the low stone walls bounding a rectangular dream. Then another spring came, and with the spring came Mr. Griffith, his young son Tommy, and his big box of tools.

I could identify Arthur Griffith as a builder, which he is, but "builder" carries connotations of subdivisions where houses come like six-packs. Mr. Griffith is cabinetmaker and master carpenter. He is a craftsman, born in Madison County in 1905, the son of a German carpenter who was in his turn the son of a German carpenter. Let me sketch him for your mind's eye: five-eight, medium weight, baggy overalls, carpenter's apron, iron-gray hair, a mustache to match. He grumbles out of habit, not out of conviction: a perfectionist. He is gruff-voiced but never grouchy. On Sundays he goes to the Lutheran Church in Culpeper. He helped to build it; and it is good. Plank by plank, beam by beam, nail by nail, Mr.

Griffith proceeded to build our dream. He had help, of course. Tommy worked all summer, until he had to go back to high school. Our own number two son Chris, home from Vietnam, gave a hand. So did number three son Kevin, who learned the hard way that laying insulation is no particular fun. Most of the time Johnny Morris was here as a cheerful first lieutenant, humming the same tune that started nowhere and went nowhere, hammering the way good carpenters hammer, letting the hammer do the work.

In early fall the Nicholson boys came, speaking the mountain speech. They finished the stone work, curving a serpentine garden wall to fit snugly on the knoll. We had Rufus Carpenter, plumber and electrician; Irving Chapman's crew, who did the plastering; the Dennises, who painted the walls and stained the rough-sawn boards outside. J. P. Dellinger, a retired railway man with a face Tom Benton would have loved to paint, rode over one day with his tractor, sprayed the land with tobacco juice, and laid the fence. Mr. Smith, the bulldozer man, carved a curving driveway.

It all went slowly. Watching Mr. Griffith, we learned that craftsmanship survives — the board that is squared and cut and fitted and cut again, and fitted and planed, and put up and taken down, and finally nailed in place at last. "Looks as if it grew there," Mr. Morris would say, nodding his head in admiration. And Mr. Griffith would say, "It'll do," or "It's not too bad." It was done by Christmas of 1969, and a happy Christmas it was.

Christmases tend to be large occasions in our household, and this was true long before we came to White Walnut Hill. The Christmas just before son Sean was fifteen, when we were living on Hanover Avenue in Richmond's Fan District, even had its own touch of country.

It was fairly late in the afternoon of December 23 when Sean, as the oldest boy, brought the tree home. They had gone out to Hanover County, he and a close friend, to a place where they "had permission," and there they had engaged in a long, judicious search through the cold and quiet woods. They had thought about bringing home a yearling pine, as a novelty, and had abandoned that idea as too much of a novelty; and finally, after two or three spruces had failed of confirmation for want of a unanimous vote, they had come across a cedar that seemed the perfect cedar.

It was in a little grove of cedars, halfway up a north slope above the stream where the two of them fished in summers, and it had the look and the shape and the air of a Christmas tree. So they felled it with an ax (a saw would have been neater, but a hundred years of custom decree that the tree must be *chopped* down, not *sawed* down), and they had dragged it down the snowy slope and across the frozen stream, stopping to inspect the thickness of the ice, which required some stomping and perilous leaping, and this had been followed by learned speculation on whether certain tracks were fox tracks or only dog tracks; but at last they had wrestled the tree into the back of a station wagon, complaining bitterly at the prickling of the needles, and what with one thing and another it was fairly late when the oldest boy brought the tree home.

Mounted in the living room, after appropriate sawing to make it stand forest straight again, the cedar seemed even larger than it had seemed in the woods, there on the slope above the stream, so that some pruning and shaping had to be done; and the middle-sized boy (this was Chris, at eleven) had to learn for himself that if you seize a cedar too firmly, you *will* get stuck; and it is not yet time, he had to be told sixteen times, to put on the tinsel; and yes, he could hang on some ornaments after the angel was made secure on top.

It was at this moment that the littlest boy (son Kevin, at eight) made the discovery.

"Look!" he cried, and his voice held pure wonder and delight. "There's a bird's nest!"

And so it was. Buried deep in the bottom branches, unnoticed in the shadows of the woods, the nest had survived snow and ice, and chopping and stomping and leaping, and being dragged and transported, and pruning and shaping, and here it was in the living room, as serenely perfect as a nest could be — three inches across and about two inches deep, formed entirely of pine tags, with small thin needles on the outside and some larger, twiggier pieces in the center; and suddenly this humble nest, in the midst of a great glitter of packages and lights and red and golden balls, made this Christmas tree quite the loveliest of them all.

It might have been a towhee's nest, or a small lark's, or a finch's or a sparrow's. Precedents and citations from an Audubon Guide proved not a great help. The littlest boy, taking a proprietary interest in the proceedings, decided the case for himself.

"It was *her* nest," he ruled, placing a stubby finger on Plate 47, and sounding out the syllables, "the in-di-go bunting's nest."

The ornithologists might have objected, but that was the nest in the cedar tree that Christmas Eve — a proud nest, occupied by an indigo bunting contrived of pipe cleaners and bright blue foil, with three blue beads where the eggs used to be, a brown cup nestled anew in green and silver branches hung with fragile scarlet fruit.

What was it that the psalmist said? "Yea, the sparrow hath found a nest for herself where she may lay her young." So was the infant laid in the manger, and so have all men sought a haven, and just so the indigo bunting that dwelled in a Christmas tree that year.

The indigo bunting's nest established a tradition. After the Grand Remove to Rappahannock, we made it a rule, once the leaves were off the trees, to scout around for each year's Christmas nest. One December — it might have been in 1973 — we had located a perfect nest in a dogwood a quarter-mile down the road toward White Walnut Run. I had intended to stop some time on my way back from Woodville and bring it in, but one forgets. Ordinarily we trim the tree on the Saturday morning before Christmas, and have the big family dinner on Sunday. Now it was Friday afternoon. The radio was forecasting "rain mixed with snow," and still no nest. "I'll get it the first thing in the morning," I promised.

The afternoon passed into darkness with no more than a fine mist seeping. We pulled the curtains, had dinner, let the fire burn low. At something after 8 o'clock, there came a peremptory knock at the kitchen door. "Lorenzo wants in," I announced. There ensued a brief combat of wills. I was reading; Marie was sewing. She ignored the knock. I opened the door, and a great white woolly sheep strolled in: Lorenzo the Magnificent. He had a clown's ball of snow on his nose. He shook gloriously, and demanded at once to go back out.

I went out with him. The dreary afternoon had become an artist's night. This was a wet and heavy snow, sticking swiftly to the fields and road. It was luminous, and it was silent. Ordinarily on such a night, you can see for miles. Now we could see for no more than fifty yards. The comfortable, familiar fences, symbols of order, tokens of security, had vanished behind a translucent milk-white curtain. Lorenzo stood motionless beside me, head high, sharing a sense of wonder.

A few hours later, on an irresistible impulse, I got back into boots and stocking cap and heavy coat. "Where are you going?" Marie asked. "To get the nest," I said. She nodded. Where else would a normally sensible man go on a snowy night just before Christmas?

My lantern thrust a beam of light through the still falling snow. Lorenzo was ecstatic. He mouthed the snow, plowing it with his black nose, tumbling with pleasure. He trotted ahead, pausing to look back now and then, and then disappeared on the road that leads to White Walnut Run. It wasn't just snow that was falling; it was snow mixed with solitude, with an absolute aloneness, with mystery and peace and pain all at the same time—the pain that goes with a bursting heart, with swollen senses that can hold no more. I remember pausing on the white and empty road to capture the snowflake moment, holding it under my tongue at midnight, while the beauty and the pain dissolved.

Lorenzo reappeared, transformed to sheep again, and we

found the nest enthroned in the dogwood tree, under a crown of snow, and brought it back for Christmas. The birds that built that nest built more than they could have known.

We don't get a white Christmas very often. Even so, Christmas in these mountains is always special. I wouldn't minimize the pleasures of Christmas in town. New York is wonderfully exciting in December. So is Chicago. Every great city has its charms—the big churches, candle-gleaming; the theaters, the stores, the Christmas windows, the sense of friendly crowds. Christmas in the country is something else. Burke's General Store in Woodville is a few light years removed from Neiman-Marcus, and you find no swarms of shoppers on the Slate Mills Road. Our churches are not cathedrals; they are God's little houses, but they too are candle-gleaming. We have none of the city's happy, honking, busy noise; but on a cold, clear Christmas Eve you can hear the church bells far away. Little else breaks the black velvet stillness — only a hound's cry, only the cracking of frost underfoot.

The crowds that we have at Christmas, come to think of it, are mostly crowds of animals and birds. The quail come skittering around like Christmas shoppers in a bargain basement, bustling after shirts here and skirts there and a sale on sweaters—or on cracked corn—down an aisle of pines.

There is a great accommodation among birds. The blue jays bounce into the bird feeders like bombers hitting a carrier deck. They dump quantities of feed on the ground, rev up their engines, and take off again. Then the sparrows and juncos and chickadees fly in to tidy up the mess. The cardinals tie Christmas ribbons in the air. We put out suet for the woodpeckers and mockingbirds; they spend their afternoons clinging to the suet tree like regular customers at Paddy's Bar, nibbling at the pretzel bowl.

The groundhogs, sensible beasts, stay home and nap, but the other animals make the rounds of Christmas parties. The rabbits go table-hopping with the chipmunks every night. During the week before Christmas, you'll often see a couple of indecisive possums trudging forlornly down the road; they have last-minute lists in their hands, but they can't find what they want, and they can't get waited on, and they have an oh-dear look on their faces.

Before the Christmas of 1976, we noticed a curious thing. We had not seen or smelled a skunk in months, but driving over to Scrabble we saw three. One was almost a pure albino— black paws, a black tip on her tail, but otherwise snow white. There's no reason to speak of this exotic creature in the feminine gender, but she looked like one of those glorious women, swathed in ermine, who step from limousines at the Plaza door. The Plaza's ladies smell better, of course, but they have the same untouchable air.

So far as human companionship is concerned, it comes down to family and a few close friends. At our own Sunday-before-Christmas dinner we can assemble one great-grand-mother, two grandparents (us), three sons, the sons' wives, three grandchildren, one beloved niece, beloved niece's two children, two sociable collies, and one visiting mutt. The mutt is too shy to join the carol singing, but the collies are in the chorus all the way. As senior grandchild, Heather distributes presents; the little ones tear up the wrapping paper; there are cries of "save the bow for next year!" At the 1976 occasion, my own happiest present came from Heather, who after Heaven knows how much patient parental coaching, stood up and spelled *Constitution* all the way through, and right the first time. The heart overflows.

Then the mob departs, and the silence tucks us in. A cardinal, Santa-scarlet, comes to the kitchen window and snares a sunflower seed. The collies stretch as collies do, their front paws flat out, their rumps up, their backs bowed, and then flop exhausted by the fire. One more Christmas. And outside, in the gathering twilight, the pure bright star hangs in the topmost branch of the silhouette oak. On such a night the reverence began. It never ends.

I got started on these recollections by remembering the

Christmas of 1969, when we moved into the new house quite literally on the heels of Arthur Griffith and Johnny Morris. They were down on hands and knees finishing the last of the kitchen flooring. The moving men stepped around them. We had moved seven times before, but never quite like that.

Meanwhile, other things had been happening. A Land Rover rolled into the driveway one day, and a handsome man dismounted as gracefully as if he were getting off a horse. He was Walker Stone, one of the great newspapermen of our time, who was in the process of retiring after seventeen years as editor-in-chief of the Scripps-Howard papers. He had heard we had bought the old Corbin place, and had dropped by to get acquainted. It was the beginning of a close friendship that a couple of years later got all the closer.

Walker was 63 when we met, a big man, not especially tall, but big-shouldered, big-boned, well-girthed. He sometimes seemed to bring the mountains right inside the house. He had a healthy head of good gray hair, and bright blue eyes, and a strong face; because he spent so much time outdoors, his face was often burned by sun or wind. He was a sportsman, hunter, world traveler; and now he was a country gentleman, squire of Hawthorn, his home eight miles away.

We had newspapering in common, and by coincidence we had something else: We were both native Oklahomans. I was born in Oklahoma City in 1920, Walker in Okemah in 1904, just three years before statehood. He never forgot his Oklahoma roots. At some point along the line, browsing around an auction sale, he came across a portrait of Alfalfa Bill Murray, the sage of Tishomingo, congressman and one-time governor. The portrait didn't exactly match the elegant decor of his living room, but he had to have it, so something else came down and the portrait went up, right above the carved marble mantel. The artist had done something to the eyes, so that Alfalfa Bill was always looking at you, skeptical, and bold, and curious, no matter where you sat in the room. Alfalfa Bill was Walker's kind of man.

Newspapering was his first, greatest, and most abiding

love. He started as a copy editor on the Washington *Daily News,* worked through the ranks, and became editor-in-chief for Scripps-Howard in 1952. His editorials were not much noted for style or erudition; they were noted for punch. He had been in the editor's chair for only a few months when Eisenhower ran for President against Stevenson. He liked Ike, but he became increasingly dismayed as September flowed into October and the general was still just coasting along. "Ike is running like a dry creek," he wrote. Coming from Walker Stone, the comment carried a special wallop that jarred the general into action. For the next 15 years, whenever they met, Eisenhower kidded him about the line.

After 42 years with Scripps-Howard, Walker retired to Rappahannock County. There he purchased Hawthorn, a 500-acre farm with a magnificent view of the Blue Ridge Mountains. The two-story brick house, white-columned, had been built around 1812 by Dr. Aylett Hawes for his beautiful young bride, Frances Thornton. She died before she could ever occupy the mansion named for the two of them. Over the generations, the property slowly ran down, but Walker fell in love with the place on a visit to Rappahannock, and set about building it up.

He raised a flagpole you could see for miles around. He threw his energies into restoring the neglected land. He always had a project going. He embarked on a venture in raising quail and pheasant, with a view toward having Hawthorn a game preserve. He loved to show off the incubators and the pens of rustling birds. At one point he decided that what Hawthorn needed was a patio—an outside sitting area where friends could have a drink and look at the ponds. By the time that project was finished he had stone terraces as massive as the courtyards of Knossos. He had another idea for raising pine trees. He loved to tinker with tools.

Anyhow, Walker invited us to come over and go fishing. He had too many yearling bass in the ponds, and wished someone would catch a couple of hundred. We promptly rigged up the fly rods, drove over to Hawthorn, and got to know Walker.

We spent many a winter evening in his library, talking politics and people and farming. His library was also the game room. Walker had hunted big game with Robert Ruark in Africa, and a dozen trophies hung from the walls. The bookshelves were jammed with a newsman's books — an undisciplined collection of biography, poetry, history, politics, law. He developed an affection for a 20-volume set of the Annals of America, and used to spend hours retrieving forgotten scraps of history.

Walker died of a massive heart attack on a Sunday afternoon in March, 1973. His death came quickly, just as he had hoped it would—a newsman's swift "30" to mark the end of a good piece of copy.

In the course of our goings and comings at Hawthorn, our number one son Sean met Walker's number one daughter Sharon. It was love all around. They announced their engagement at a bang-up Fourth of July party in 1969, got married in October, and the following July produced our number one granddaughter Heather. Sean and Sharon have minds of their own. They were married in the Baptist church down in Sperryville, but they wrote their own vows. This is what she said (and he repeated) as they stood face to face, holding hands:

> *In the presence of God and these our friends, I, Sharon, take thee, Sean, to be my lawfully wedded husband, promising to be unto thee a loving and faithful wife, so long as we both shall live.*

That was it. Cousin Michael Allen Nestor, who used to play in the brass section of the Richmond Symphony, had come to Rappahannock for the occasion. He lifted his golden horn in Purcell's "Trumpet Voluntary." You could hear it all the way to the Exxon station. Then Sean got into kilts of the Clan Colquhoun, and the happy couple headed for the Boar's Head Inn in Charlottesville on their honeymoon. As I said, Heather was born the following July, which tells you something about the wearing of kilts.

Norman Isaacs, who spent many years with the Louisville *Courier-Journal* and moved late in life to the Wilmington *News*, once explained to me why grandparents and grand-children get to be so close: They share a common hostility. Be that as it may, Heather moved instantly into our hearts. In July of 1971, I wrote a column in the form of a letter to her:

Dear Heather:

At this very hour, minute and second of the 20th Century, you are standing free and clear in your playpen on the deck of your grandfather's house, which is located four miles from Scrabble, in Rappahannock County, Commonwealth of Virginia, United States of America, Planet Earth. You will be one year old tomorrow. And your pants are wet.

You ought not to be embarrassed, years hence, to have this entirely natural circumstance recorded. There are times when the whole country, come to think of it, seems to be enduring the same condition—a kind of vague discomfort, not wholly understood. But at least you have a mother to snatch you up, pat you dry, kiss your nose, and plop you back down in the playpen, all in less time than it takes me to change a typewriter ribbon. The country is not so lucky.

To continue: You now stand about three inches taller than the top of your playpen, and this is a good thing because it permits you to chew on its edge without seriously bending your neck. You have eight teeth. You have the most beautiful black-rimmed blue eyes this side of Killarney, and at last, praise God, you are growing a perfectly senatorial ducktail. Every time you frown, you remind me of Tom Connally calling on his colleagues to restrict the World Court.

This is, at age one, a time of discovery. In the

past ten minutes, since you returned dry-pantsed, you have discovered, in addition to the taste of foam rubber: An ant, your left hand, Lorenzo's nose, the feel of fur, sunlight on your arm, and a hummingbird poised on a butterfly bush. You have discussed all this with Lorenzo. He is not very interested, if the truth were known, but he wants what remains of your cookie.

You are making other discoveries, outside the playpen, not quite so pleasant. You are discovering that steps are hard, when you fall down two or three of them; and you are discovering that if you insist on exploring the cabinet where the soap powder is kept, you will likely get slapped on the hand. Useful lessons, these, for grand-daughters and for Presidents alike.

You are not yet walking, but you can crawl from a crouching start to 42 miles per hour in 11 seconds flat. You are showing bookish instincts. Earlier in the afternoon, you pulled out a bottom shelf of books all the way from Carlyle to Chaucer; it was an act that gave your grand-father great pleasure; he had forgotten Carlyle altogether.

"Happy the people whose annals are blank in history-books." That was Carlyle for you. And perhaps the converse of the proposition contains an equal truth. It is the wet pants syndrome. Whatever may be said of your first year of life, it has offered more than blank pages of history—a war we did not want to get into but could not stay out of; a host of racial problems of uncertain beginnings and unforeseeable endings; prob-lems of discipline, problems of money, problems of prices, problems that were all our own fault but not exactly our own fault. We are not, in 1971, an especially happy people; and the pages of history are jammed.

But right now, at age one, you are as indifferent to history as Lorenzo the Magnificent, who is licking your face with a great rough tongue. This enchants you. Your nose is crinkled and your eyes are shut; you are standing on tiptoe, beauty and the beast, crumbs and pure delight—and all of Heather's world begins and ends with a collie's nose. Neither one of you cares whether Nixon goes to China.

A couple of spinnaker clouds are tacking slowly by Turkey Mountain. It is pleasant to speculate on the history of 1971 that will indeed matter to Heather in high school, to Heather at century's end. Your grandfather is a poor prophet, and there are times when he doubts the Western world has the will to preserve your inheritance, but for the record: The most significant pages of our history will deal not with war or statecraft, but with biology — the biology of genetics, the secrets of life. It is a cool thought for a sunny afternoon, but Heather, my love, life is more than hummingbirds' tongues and collies' noses. We will take up the topic anew next year, when you are a talkative two.

Love,
Grandfather

Well, Heather did get to be a talkative two—and a talkative three, and four, and five, and six. I fell into the practice of writing a column in the form of a letter to her every year, and these columns churned up such a lively response I have included them, *seriatim*, at the end of the book. It is astounding how many people have daughters or granddaughters born in the summer of 1970.

In September of 1973 Heather acquired a brother, Douglas Stone, and chattered the little fellow practically into silence. A couple of years later, in April of 1976, she acquired a cousin Alina, born to son Chris and his actress wife Gina. It is a tender and touching experience, I can tell you, to watch a six-year-old giving a bottle to a six-month-old — the infant madonna and child. The arrival of Alina was a pinnacle for Heather; she encountered her share of pitfalls, too.

When the Grand Remove to Rappahannock began, that Sunday morning back in 1966, we were thinking only in terms of a remodeled cottage for weekend use. No sooner was work completed on the cottage than Marie's studio had to be built. Once the studio was built, we began to dream of the main house. When we moved into the main house, we said: This is it. No more construction. *Finis!*

But it became evident, after a while, that I had to have a better place to work in. I was trying to write in a roomy alcove off my bedroom. This was all right, in a way — I had book-shelves, a big desk, a couple of filing cabinets, a sturdy stand for my old rimfire Underwood—but it wasn't really all right. By this time we had sold the little place on G Street, Southeast, ignoring the surly complaints of Sullivan the cat, and had acquired a townhouse in Old Town Alexandria. I was spending half my time there and half at home in Rappahannock, and the files and books I needed were always at the other place.

So we began to look at the cottage anew. If we took out a window on the east wall, and turned it into a door; and if we extended the back porch another eight or ten feet; and if we worked a roof line this way . . . This was the summer of 1973, and Arthur Griffith wasn't available; he was building a house for someone else down in Culpeper. We turned to Peter Kramer, a capable young cabinetmaker in little Washington. Peter drew up some plans, and before long we were knee-deep again in sawdust, shavings, and stonemason's chips.

This was my own dream come true. Back around 1935 or 1936, when I was a boy growing up in Oklahoma City, the Duesenberg people were advertising their elegant cars in some elegant full-page ads in the slick magazines. One ad showed a haughty woman standing with a haughty grey-hound: "She Drives a Duesenberg." Another ad—and this is the one that stuck in my head for thirty-odd years—showed a distinguished gentleman in smoking jacket, standing by his desk in a stunning library: "He Drives a Duesenberg." As a boy I didn't dream of a Duesenberg — not much, anyhow; but, Dear Lord, I dreamed of that library.

The idea was for Peter Kramer to build something like it, adapted to the hills of Rappahannock County and to the humble planks of the Corbin cottage. I wanted room for 3,500 books. I wanted room for hundreds of magazines and for great heaps of newspapers. I wanted file drawers; I wanted special places for big dictionaries and great thick atlases; I wanted lamps to gleam on the red and black bindings of Supreme Court Reports. Writers live by what other writers write; we feed on the written word like cows on a stack of hay. The insatiable reader is just that: insatiable. Deprived of something to read, he declines; he fidgets, he sighs. A writer could exist, I suppose without books around him, but it would be an awful existence.

As it turned out, the finished library was something short of the Duesenberg library, but it was close enough for comfort. Peter built me an office 16 x 28. He brought in Joe Caliandro to serve as foreman, principal mason, and boss of the whole shebang. Joe was a pure delight. He was short, handsome, dark-eyed, dark-haired, a voluble Italian-American with a mousetrap temper. Though he was only in his mid-thirties, he had been through one of those fearful heart operations that leave a massive scar behind. He refused to work at a moderate pace. Full throttle, that was Joe. He was alternately joyous and despondent, all the way up or all the way down. He drove himself as if he were driving a Ferrari, right up to ten-tenths of what the machine could do. The assorted carpenters, plumbers, electricians, roofers, painters and mortar mixers who labored under Joe's impassioned command never knew quite what to make of him. He was a sawed-off Fellini; he was author, producer, director, *primo maestro.* Once he dressed down his crew with a profane eloquence that left them open-mouthed. He waved, he shouted, he held his nose, he rolled his eyes, he curled his lip, he spat, he clenched his fists, he mixed his dog Italian with polemic English. "Joe," I said, when the crew had crept away, "that was quite a performance."

"Cast of thousands," he said. And grinned.

We got very close to Joe Caliandro in the six months that he spent around the place, building the office, laying some stone walks and walls, gabbing when the day's work was done. In January of 1974 he went back to Cleveland for a second heart operation. He was full of bravado, and sick with premonitions also. The premonitions were sound. He died on the operating table of a massive hemorrhage that could not be stanched. They buried him in a little country cemetery down near Riva, where his wife's people had come from. The eulogy came from II Timothy: "I have fought a good fight, I have finished my course, I have kept the faith." His crew, scarcely recognizable in dark suits and shirts and ties, stood by the grave and wept.

The final stage of the Grand Remove took place in October 1973. We sold the townhouse in Old Town, summoned a massive moving van, and hauled sixteen tons of stuff to White Walnut Hill. The townhouse had been a pleasant place, blessed by the presence of two beloved ladies, Alice and Courtney, who occupied the fourth floor, and it had served as my Washington base for more than five years. Alexandria's Old Town, I remark in passing, ranks among the most charming neighborhoods in America. It has none of Georgetown's desperate quest for putting-on-the-dog. In Old Town, strangers still nod and murmur when they pass on the narrow sidewalks. We were sorry to give it up.

Life is a constant process of endings and beginnings, all flowing together. Working, playing, eating, sleeping, meeting deadlines, reading a book, taking a trip—these are all starts and finishes — but the act of moving from one domicile to another has particular meaning. Like graduation, or marriage, or the birth of a child, or death in the family, moving is a pivot point. Even with the same furnishings, nothing is exactly the same thereafter. Moving means going to another *place,* and if you have a strong sense of place, a love of roots, the act of getting yourself transplanted costs a pang.

To be sure, moving has its happier aspects also. Before the boxcar van arrived, Marie and I spent two days at hard labor over the packing boxes. We marveled, as we always do on such occasions, at the amount of sheer junk — sheer stuff! — that somehow accumulates. They say that a love of property is rooted in the conservative philosophy, but a love for jelly glasses? For souvenirs of Atlantic City? For last year's Congressional Record? The Princess Street townhouse had a tremendous attic and two dozen closets, and we had been reared in the magpie school of Never Throw Anything Away. It might come in handy some time. Coat hangers, shirt cardboards, pencil stubs, old playing cards, moth-eaten sweaters. Out with them all!

Packing up books is the hardest task. The truly bookish fellow acquires books in tumbleweed fashion; he is forever picking up a few more as he rolls along. He tends to forget what he has. The packing-up process thus becomes a period of rediscovery. One sits cross-legged on the floor, reveling in a precious find. Hey, look! Housman! And the packing-up process tends to get suspended for a time.

It was done at last — the floors swept, the heavy cartons loaded, the keys turned over to the real estate man. We waved the van away, uncorked a bottle of wine, and sat on the steps sipping from salvaged jelly glasses. In the cool October twilight, my thoughts turned again to the theme of endings and beginnings. The move from Old Town marked an end, the new office a beginning. Professionally, it meant a turning point. To live physically in Washington, if you happen to be a newsman, is the power and the glory. To live only minutes away from where the action is, to lunch with the high and mighty, to share in the crystal glitter of Embassy Row—all this has great allure. Washington, for my own taste, is the most beautiful capital in the world; the city is exciting, fascinating, stimulating, and exhausting. If it lacks Broadway, Times Square, and major league ball, well, the real-life Senators are funnier and sadder than their diamond counterparts used to be. Washington offers all an editorial columnist could ask.

Everything but perspective. I have a notion that Presidents must feel the same lack, which is why they leave town so often. Washington is a great place for doing — for acting, achieving, moving and shaking. The capital is always one fine active verb; the city is constantly meeting, voting, hearing, deciding, confirming, passing, rejecting, sustaining, overriding, conniving, quarreling, splitting, confronting, and joining. Washington is perfect for all these things, but it is not much of a place for thinking. In my own case, I had begun to feel an urgent need for perspective—for the vision that keeps foreground, middle distance and background in orderly arrangement. I had snubbed my nose so firmly to the passing hour, staring through a blurred windowpane at political events, that I was losing sight of history's infinite Big Parade.

It is hard to explain these things. But I knew, when we put the jelly glasses down and tossed the empty wine bottle in the last green plastic bag of trash, I knew the ending and the beginning were right. We drove in contented silence back to White Walnut Hill, and a few days later the books and I were snuggled down in the lamplit library that Peter Kramer built, at the end of Caliandro's walk.

There was a pang or two, as I said, about selling the Alexandria townhouse, for it had proved a wonderfully pleasant base for Washington operations. The sale produced another pang also—the pang of a guilty conscience. Our real estate agent sold the house for a walloping sum of money. One of these days the figures may be of antiquarian interest: We bought the house in the fall of 1968 for $44,000, and sold it just five years later for $81,000. That is inflation for you. To be sure, by the time the grandchildren grow up, the same eight-room house may be selling for $181,000. Who knows? But in the autumn of 1973, even after a capital gains tax, we found ourselves delightfully solvent, with the new office paid for and no more than a moderately horrendous mortgage on White Walnut Hill. The column was doing well; I was getting more deeply into television; my agent was commanding lecture fees that struck me as just short of scandalous. In working up our income tax for calendar 1973, I was rendered speechless by the evidence that I myself, beating on the rimfire Underwood, was paying enough in taxes to underwrite the whole of the salary of a United States Senator. A more depressing thought seldom occurs.

It was time to Do Something about this state of affairs. I happened to be flying from San Francisco to Denver, or from somewhere to somewhere, and ran out of store-bought things to read. A compulsive reader will read *anything.* After I had exhausted the resources of the seat card, explaining the oxygen system, I dug into the seat pocket for United's own magazine. There was a piece about the tax and retirement advantages that accrue to professionals who incorporate themselves. It sounded peachy-keen. Thousands of veterinarians, lawyers, doctors, dentists, opticians, and the like had turned themselves into peecees, or Personal Corporations. These fellows weren't supporting Senators; they were supporting their own eventual retirement. One of my brother pundits, Carl Rowan, had gone the corporate route. He used to be a barefoot Tennessee boy with nothing in his pocket but a couple of old copy pencils. Now he had taken to inc. I asked him how he liked it. "When you address me on these matters," he said loftily, "you may address me as 'Mr. President.'"

In the course of a few months, after the lawyers, accountants and pension consultants had done their work, I became us. Or it. We are a Virginia corporation with a black satchel full of stock certificates to prove it. The certificates are printed in marmalade orange. Our vice president picked out the color to match a new dress she bought for the first directors' meeting. We also have a Great Corporate Seal that granddaughter Heather loves to play with. We have a Minute Book. We have a thousand forms to fill in. We have a Money Purchase Pension Trust that only God and Frank Gentile understand, Mr. Gentile being the man from New York Life. We are in-cor-por-a-ted, in the first person plural, but in the first person singular I can tell you: It ain't no bed of roses.

Being "Mr. President" isn't so bad. The miserable part is that as the corporation's chief executive officer, I am now working for *them*. After eight years of giddy freedom, I found myself back on a corporate payroll again. Gone, the carefree days! Gone, the windfall piece of cash! We had been us for only a month when I ran out of walking-around money and had to get an advance on expenses. It seemed ridiculous for we to sign a check made out to us, so we asked Virginia Swaim, the Secretary-Treasurer, to sign a check instead. She turned the voucher over two or three times and gave me the cool look of a downtown banker.

"Well," she said, disapproval written large upon her lovely forehead, "that's an awful lot of money you're asking for."

"Yeah," we said, "but look, Jinnie, it's, uh, only a temporary kind of —"

Her pen paused over the checkbook. "How long have you been with the corporation?" she asked.

She finally relented, and disgorged the advance, but it was a struggle. Everything in corporate life is a struggle. You have to have regular meetings of the stockholders. Believe me, stockholders are nothing but trouble. We held our first stockholders' meeting, and all two of them came.

"Where's the box lunch?" demanded a voice from the rear of the room.

"Now, darling," we said.

"Don't darling me," said the heckler. "This must be a pretty sorry corporation if you don't even have a box lunch for the stockholders."

We took a recess, made three ham-and-cheese on rye, and the meeting resumed.

"What about a dividend?" the same voice wanted to know. "What about an informative annual report? And how come with all that salary you need such a pension?"

"Look, honey," said the president of the corporation. "In today's competitive market for top executive talent, it is imperative that pension benefits be provided that are commensurate with revenue production and income flow."

"That's what all you overpaid fat cats say," sneered the usually tender voice. "Besides, you forgot the pickle on the sandwich."

In addition to the marmalade certificates, the corporate seal, and the minute book, we have a flock of tax forms. Unless you run a small business, you cannot imagine the tax forms. Our little peecee had scarcely organized before the heavens opened and the forms came raining down. For a while we had not one Employer Number, but by inadvertence, *two*. This drove the IRS computers mad. These particular computers live in Memphis, where they occupy a tremendous windowless building, half a mile square and a quarter mile high. Here the hand of man, as they say, has never set foot; no human voice is ever heard. All incoming mail is mechanically opened, scanned, and routed by conveyor belt to computers and robot typewriters. The poor fellow with *two* Employer Numbers, instead of one, gets the Reply Chilly, followed by the Reply Intimidating, followed by the Response Ugly, followed by the Threat Explicit. The computers cannot be appealed to, reasoned with, or kidded along. It took eight months to get the surplus number cancelled. If it ever was cancelled.

The corporate life also involves balance sheets, operating statements, quarterly meetings, waivers of notice, and the payment of walloping taxes by the third business day of every month. A properly managed peecee earns no net income and declares no dividends; mainly it fills in forms. So we don't know about us. We are the only known corporation with a home office in Scrabble, Virginia, and if it wouldn't take six months, two lawyers, three accountants, and five computers to dissolve us, by George, we would let the distinction go.

Now and then readers write in to ask how I like the whole business of living and working at home, 80 miles from Washington. I write back and say, fine. Sure, there are some disadvantages. Now and then I miss the sense of *presence,* of being physically on the scene when a committee hearing erupts, or the Supreme Court hands down a hot opinion, or a couple of Senators go at it on the floor. But when I'm not on the road, lecturing or covering a story, I spend two days a week in Washington; and two days are enough. The schedule tends to keep friendly politicians at arm's length, which is the best possible place for them. I do my television stints, touch base at the Washington *Star,* pick up mail and messages, harvest a bushel of things that have to be read; and late on Friday afternoons, I head down the highway for home.

West of Warrenton, the traffic thins out. In winter it's too dark to see much of anything, but from March through November the Virginia countryside unrolls and the Blue Ridge Mountains lie in silhouette against the setting sun. In spring the land is painted in pastels—in watercolor tints of green and white and beige. In fall the canvas is much bolder; the gothic trees frame stained glass windows to a windswept sky. The ribbon road winds on past Amissville and little Washington. Then it leads, narrower now, and graveled, back into the woods and the hills; across the Thornton River, past Manwaring's well-kept pastures, around a steep curve and up and down — and there are the lamps of home. The collies come racing along the fence line, barking a furious welcome, thrusting insistent noses to be nuzzled. And through the opening door, love.

Part Two

Which is mostly about
Rappahannock County and a few
Rappahannockers.

A long in the late summer of 1973, a letter turned up in the mailbox. The letter raised certain questions of ethics, honesty, veracity, and wise public policy. These are among the great issues that, up in the mountains, we think about all the time.

The letter came from a woman living on San Antonio Avenue in Menlo Park, California. It was addressed (and the address presented, as they say, some threshold problems) to "Chamber of Commerce, Scrabble, Va." It read, in full:

> Dear Sir:
>
> Will you send me information re your city — housing, temperature, rainfall, cultural activities, everything you have. I am seeking a good place to retire to.
>
> Thank you.

You may well ask how this interesting inquiry fell into my hands, inasmuch as there is no city of Scrabble, Virginia, and if there were a city of Scrabble, we would have no Chamber of Commerce. Commerce is one thing we are positively against in these parts. The liveliest commerce we have around here comes when Sheriff John Walker Jenkins puts on an auction, and that is not exactly commerce. It is more of a social occasion. For the record, I should say that John Walker is not sheriff any more. He was defeated for reelection in 1975 by Trooper Buntin, but in Virginia, public titles are for life. We still call John Walker sheriff. He's a fine auctioneer.

In any event, the letter from Menlo Park found its way to the Woodville Rural Independent Post Office, Zip Code 22749, headed by Mrs. Ruth Orange, postmistress. The Post Office is a one-room wooden structure, furnished with a sitting bench, a rocking chair, and a potbellied stove. A slender partition separates the sitting area from the working area. Now and then Mrs. Orange puts up a poster warning aliens about registration, or she decorates the partition with a flyer for duck stamps, but we have no aliens and very few ducks. We did have an alien once. He was an amiable Korean by the name of Han, who occupied the tenant house over at Walker Stone's place and grew Korean vegetables there. He used to cater local cocktail parties. His egg rolls were works of oriental art. Han also gained a certain fame when he forgot to set the brakes on Walker's Jeep, and the Jeep rolled into the fishpond. Everybody liked Han, but the Jeep was a mess.

I was talking about the Woodville Rural Independent Post Office. The sitting area often is occupied by Lacy Orange, who is Mrs. Orange's husband, and by Clifton Clark, who lives down the Rudasill's Mill Road and raises hounds for fox hunting. Mr. Clark buys dog food in 50-pound bags, about 20 bags at a time, and the bags are stacked near the sitting bench. When Jake Sisk drops by, or some of the Johnson brothers come in, or H. B. Wood pauses to pass the time of day, someone has to sit on the dog food bags. They sit pretty good. Jake lives next door to the Post Office, in a little white building that used to be a service station years ago. He is 70 years old, give or take a few years. He refinishes chairs and tables to pick up some spending money. Jake painted the inside of the plate glass windows in his house with white paint, and then scratched out a few peepholes. It's a startling experience, walking away from the Post Office, to glance at Jake's place and to see a bloodshot eye rolling suspiciously around a peephole. It's old Jake, keeping an eye on things.

Mrs. Orange put the letter from Menlo Park in with my mail because I use Scrabble as the dateline for my occasional country columns. I have been known to tell some stretchers in these bucolic dispatches, and Mrs. Orange figured the Scrabble Chamber of Commerce was my invention.

The first question about this letter was, should it even be opened? It was a nice ethical question, even a nice legal question. Who am I to open mail addressed to nonexistent chambers of commerce in nonexistent cities? Curiosity fought with propriety, and as you will have deduced already, curiosity won. The larger questions then arose. Should the letter be answered at all? Elementary courtesy was thought to demand a reply of some sort. But should the letter be answered honestly? This was the sticker. On the one hand, telling the truth would cause nothing but trouble. If I were honestly to describe Scrabble, and more broadly to write about Rappahannock County, word of our unsullied paradise would spread far and wide. We would be invaded by legions of Californians seeking a good place to retire in. Pretty soon would come the sub-dividers, paving roads and selling lots in Scrabble Heights, Scrabble Cliffs, and Scrabble Manor. In the wake of the real estate promoters would come Little Leagues, supermarkets, and chintzy shoppes calling themselves Ye Olde. Once the truth got out, nothing of value would remain.

On the other hand, how could a Southerner lie to a lady in Menlo Park? No way. So I wrote to this effect:

First off, though Scrabble is not a city, a town, or even a village, Scrabble most certainly *is*. Some of my skeptical readers, off and on through the years, have had the nerve to suggest that Scrabble does not exist; that it is a mere invention, a myth, a device, a literary land somewhere north of Yoknapatawpha County and somewhat west of Camelot or Middle Earth. The charge is wholly without merit.

The community known as Scrabble sleeps some 13 miles west of Culpeper, Virginia, just off Route 522 in Rappahannock County, on the eastern slopes of the Blue Ridge Mountains. In general, Scrabble embraces the area between Turkey Ridge and Bessie Bell Mountain. There is nothing much in this area. The largest structure is the Mt. Lebanon Baptist Church (founded 1833). Commerce is represented by a saw-mill and by Dennis's Store on Route 626. If you keep going up 626 you get to Rock Mills. There is nothing much there, either. You will find Scrabble on Civil War maps, sometimes under the name of Hardscrabble, and you will find it to this day on the Sperryville Quadrangle of the Geological Survey and on the official State Highway Department map of Rappahannock County. Scrabble had its own Post Office until Mr. Farley economized it out of existence in 1937. There used to be a two-room Scrabble School and even a Scrabble Gift Shop. The abandoned school yard now houses the Scrabble Dump, where I take the non-burnable trash every Saturday morning, and the gift shop is out of business. Except for the church, the dump, the sawmill and the store, nobody thinks much about Scrabble except to remember that Scrabble is where you turn if you're going up to Homer Henry's to play softball. Anyhow, as I was saying, there's nothing make-believe about it. Scrabble really-o, truly-o, *is.* It just isn't much.

Ephemeral though its population and boundary may be, Scrabble slumbers contentedly in the southern tip of a contented county. Our history, such as it is, goes back to the time in 1740 when Francis Thornton explored our mountains and found them good. He brought his family here—the county still is full of Thorntons — and the road from Madison to Sperryville is known to this day as the F. T. Valley Road. George Washington was here, of course. He laid out the town that in 1796 would be named in his honor, and he gave its main street the name of Gay Street after his sweetheart, Gay Fairfax. It was about what you would expect of a 17-year-old boy.

The town of Washington prospered, became a courthouse town, acquired Cox's Hotel. They say that the venerable George, just before he got to be President, danced in Cox's dining room. But as the years passed, the community stopped growing. It sat down, resting easy, with its back against the mountains. For the past 150 years, more or less, the biggest excitement in little Washington, except for court days, has been watching the peaches grow.

Rappahannock County got to be a county, officially speaking, in 1833. It first appears in the census of 1840 with a population of 9,259. We peaked at 9,782 in 1850, and except for one brief spurt between 1880 and 1890, the population has dropped in every decennial census since that time. It makes a man quietly proud. By 1970 we were down to 5,199, which gave us a density of 19 persons per square mile. That is just about exactly right. In 1972 one of the planning agencies at the State capital down in Richmond hired some high-toned consultants to make county-by-county projections of anticipated population changes. The consultants licked their pencils and figured Rappahannock would be down to 5,100 by 1990, off by another two per cent. The headline on page one of the Rappahannock *News* told the story as Rappahannockers saw it: "Favorable Population Trend Seen."

As of 1971, we were 4,340 white and 850 nonwhite; we were almost precisely 50 per cent male and 50 per cent female, a nice arrangement. Median age, 31.0 years; median education, 7.9 school years; median family income, $6,077. It doesn't show up in demographic analysis, but we also are divided into Old Rappahannockers and Outlanders. In between the two communities is a gulf of income, life-style, and remembered experience. The Outlanders embrace all those city fellows who have bought land in recent years — active airline pilots, flying out of Dulles; retired officers of the Army and Navy; an investment banker, a scattering of journalists. The Outlanders are subdivided into full-timers and weekenders. The social doings of even the full-timers are not reported in the Rappahannock *News;* such weekenders as Rowland Evans, David Brinkley and Bill Monroe, however famed they may be in the Great Beyond, are mere exotic birds of passage in Scrabble, Slate Mills and Flint Hill. Now and then an Outlander successfully traverses the gulf. Ian Pryde, who used to be a fireman in New Jersey, became a top man in the rescue squad. The late Frank McGee of NBC, who farmed a big spread near Long Mountain, was one of the Saturday morning boys at the Farmers' Co-op. Not many Outlanders make it.

The Old Rappahannockers have been here practically forever. Early in the Nineteenth Century, a census taker found such families as Thornton, Miller, Fletcher, Meade, Slaughter, Strother, Wood, Lane, French, Green, Shackelford, Mason, Turner, Nalle, Amiss, Browning, Moffett, Thompson, Snead, Carter, Gordon, Johnson, Rudasill, O'Bannon, Botts, and Lewis. They're still here. They are like rings in the stump of a tree; they mark the county's age.

Continuity. Rappahannockers are great ones for continuity. Families remain; place names echo long-gone generations; the mountains never change. Our mountains are not the pushy, spectacular, show-off mountains of the Sierras, the Rockies, or the Swiss Alps. Nobody ever would confuse the Blue Ridge with the Himalayas. Ours are comfortable mountains, nicely rounded, never bony; they are not meant to be attacked; they are meant to be lived with.

White Walnut Hill lists an elevation of 620 feet. We look at Red Oak, with 1120. The highest mountain I can think of, until you get in the Blue Ridge proper, is Jenkins Mountain at 2024. Some of our mountains come in families—Jenkins and Little Jenkins, Mason and Little Mason, Battle and Little Battle, Big Mulky and Little Mulky. Once I saw an ad in the Rappahannock *News* for a cabin offered for sale on Big Bastard Mountain, but I never could find this pinnacle on the map. I think someone made it up.

Mountains we have — mountains, and ridges, and hills — and in between are the hollows: Harris Hollow and Jenkins Hollow and Devil's Hollow. For a mile or so below Sperryville, the Thornton River is a bit polluted. Otherwise the streams run crystal clear — the Hazel, the Hughes, the Jordan, the Rush. In the old days every river had its mill, and the county still is dotted with communities that recall another age: Slate Mills, Rock Mills, Laurel Mills, Peola Mills. If the truth must be told, the air is as pure as the water; except for the chimney smoke that spirals from our houses in winter, nothing mars the placid skies. Our red clay soil, if you treat it friendly, produces two-pound tomatoes and squash the size of beach balls. We grow corn so tenderhearted that it cries to be eaten. Our black-eyed peas are works of the jeweler's art.

As for the temperature, we have just enough variety and very few extremes. It gets below zero once or twice a winter; it climbs to 90 a few times in July. The rainfall is about right. It rarely rains for weddings, auctions, church socials, or hunt days, but it rains gently on sleepy Sunday afternoons. Now and then we have flash floods that tear up the gravel roads and sweep away the bridge railings, but the Lord provides these mainly to give us something to talk about.

The lady in Menlo Park asked about cultural activities.

These we have in abundance. We have a firemen's carnival every weekend in August; we have hog killings in November, and we have eight to ten revivals every year. We have quilting bees, turkey shoots, all-day apple butter socials, and a livestock auction every Thursday at Front Royal. That is all the culture we are up to. Rappahannockers figure that anyone who is desperate for culture can go into Culpeper to a movie, or drive down to the University in Charlottesville, or even succumb to the high-toned temptations of Washington, D. C. We have a fine little library at the county seat and a reliable weekly paper in the Rappahannock *News*. Anyone who needs more reading material can always go to the Woodville Rural Independent Post Office and read the warning to resident aliens.

So much for the metes and bounds and vital statistics of Rappahannock County. As spokesman for the Scrabble Chamber of Non-Commerce, I perhaps should add that of honest industry, we have none. Whenever some heretic arises to say that industry should be invited in, an *ad hoc* committee forms to keep the industry out. Of dishonest industry, we have very little; back in the hollows, along those limpid runs, hot mash is cooled by crystal waters, but the art dies. People do work in Rappahannock. In season, they work hard, making hay, tending orchards, raising cattle, mending fences, but they never work so hard they forget when the fish are rising or the hounds are running or the deer are grazing on Grindstone Mountain.

All this is the truth. I'm sorry now that I wrote it down.

Thinking about work, I'm reminded again of Charlie Settle. God rest him. He was an Independent American, and they are rare birds in our time. He stood just under six feet tall, slim as a pole bean, with a long, sad face that always looked as if he'd just slept in it. His teeth were terrible — half of them missing, and those that were left, dark-stained — but you forgot all that when he smiled. It was the happiest, slowest,

50

most satisfied smile you ever saw. Charlie had the right attitude about work. He worked when he felt like working; and he didn't work when he had something better to do.

We were put on to Charlie by Mr. Weldon Burke, the patriarch of Scrabble district who owns the general store and Exxon station at Woodville. This was when we first came to Rappahannock. Mr. Burke is red-faced and white-haired, and he wears sunglasses all year long. He peered at us over the counter next to the cash register, understood that we were strangers, and gave us our first lesson in country manners. We had said respectfully that we wanted to hire someone to get a few things done.

"You look up Charlie Settle," said Mr. Burke. "He's working on a stone wall down the Slate Mills Road. But don't say you want to 'hire' him. You ask if he'll he'p you."

So we drove down the Slate Mills Road, sun-drenched in an April morning, the dogwoods white and the streams lace ruffled, and sure enough, Charlie was working on the wall. He didn't look up; he just kept laying stones. It took twenty minutes of exploratory conversation—the winter past, the spring present, the art of building walls, the hopes of the Baltimore Orioles—before the delicate subject of employment could be broached. Could he he'p us? Evidently we passed muster. We had committed no gross improprieties, such as talking actual money. We emanated no aura of time clocks, warranties, low bids, firm estimates, or taxes withheld. He looked us over. "Yep," he said at last, he would come on a Tuesday and see what he could do.

As it turned out, Charlie could do anything. He could paint a house, frame a door, pour concrete, patch a roof. He could lay bricks, spread linoleum, run a wire, prune a tree. He could plow a garden, string a fence, ditch a road. There is an art to splitting logs; Charlie knew it. There is a way of rolling stones, using the weight of the rock against the rock itself; Charlie knew it. He could kill a hog, tend bees, set a trap, put poison in a groundhog hole. He could spread gravel, move dirt, mow weeds, and doctor an ailing motor. He was a master at build-

51

ing walls of stone. He was the one who operated on our sad, anemic springs and made them well again.

Charlie fixed his own wages: Two dollars an hour, flat. That might be enough, we said, for cutting grass, but it was far too low for the mason's art. On skilled jobs, we wanted to raise his pay. Charlie would not be budged. If he made more money, he'd start to worry about it; he'd get tied down to *property;* pretty soon he'd be borrowing from the bank, and he'd have payments to make. Then he'd *have* to work. Damned if that was any life for a free man. So Charlie fixed his hours, too. He would show up for three or four days, then go fishing, or putter around his own place, or work for someone else in greater need. He was a free man.

He used to roar around Rappahannock County in an ancient pickup truck, swaying like a stagecoach, with a devoted mutt named Ringo riding shotgun at his side. He knew every hollow, every house, every moonshine still, every covey of quail. He knew his people. Once at the end of a working day, we asked about locking up the tools overnight. We thought they might be stolen. Charlie scoffed at the notion. Nobody in Rappahannock County, he said, ever stole anything he might have to work with.

Charlie's formal education, you might say, was not extensive. He had briefly attended a one-room school some forty years earlier, just long enough to master rudimentary reading and his numbers, but there his book-learning stopped. Late on Saturday evenings, over a can of beer, we would compute his week's wages by adding his daily hours. "Two eights," he would say, "one four-and-a-half, and one nine-and-a-quarter." It sufficed. He knew the higher mathematics of moons for hunting 'coon and stars for planting corn. He knew how to take honey from a hive and water from a stone.

Charlie was the last man on earth you would have picked for a heart attack, but in January of 1968, working on a spring near Castleton, the shovel fell from his hands and he was dead in an hour. They buried him from the Baptist Church in Woodville, and put him to rest in the hills. After that we hired

52

city people from Culpeper and Front Royal and Warrenton, competent men with power tools and bill forms and numbers in the yellow pages, but except for such craftsmen as Arthur Griffith, it wasn't the same. Down at the foot of White Walnut Hill, close by the stream, is a springhouse built of stone. It is, in its way, a work of art, perfectly proportioned, built for the ages. The cement cap bears a proud inscription: "C. Settle, 1966." Michelangelo never did anything better.

Charlie's attitude toward work was entirely characteristic of the attitude evinced by Rappahannockers generally: Take it or leave it. As one consequence, the county tends to stay poor but proud. Such stubborn inde-by-damn-pendence could not indefinitely escape the notice of those who find dependence more to their liking. Back in 1968, the Great World Outside (by which is meant the world east of Warrenton) intruded upon this peaceful way of life. We got hit by the Poverty Program.

It caused a considerable stir. No event since the tornado of 1927 aroused so much commotion. The Federal Government had begun giving away food about 1935, but Rappahannock had never officially participated in the programs. It was a matter of principle. Self-reliance! Stand on your own two feet! God helps them that help themselves! Old doctrines are like old mountains: You get used to living with them.

But early in 1968, the United States Department of Agriculture ran a flock of figures through its computers. After a while a deplorable fact emerged: Forty-four counties in the United States were hardcore holdouts from the Poverty Program. Their refusal to accept free food for distribution became a sore point with what was known as the Poor People's Campaign. These were the folks who set up Resurrection City in the muddy Mall of Washington that spring. The PPC put pressure on the USDA. Maybe the White House put the arm on Secretary Freeman. In any event, orders went out that the recalcitrant 44 were to be whipped into line. Among the 44 was Rappahannock County, Virginia. The regional office in

Atlanta got the word. The first anyone knew of all this locally was around the first of May. It was just after the Deep Run races and just before the Warrenton Gold Cup races, which always coincide with Kentucky Derby Day; our minds were not on poor folks and poverty, but on more important matters —on a couple of horses, now forgotten, named Dancer's Image and Forward Pass. It is important in Rappahannock County to keep one's priorities straight: Animals first, people second. It was on the Thursday before Derby Day that Newbill Miller got the letter from Atlanta. Newbill was then chairman of our board of supervisors.

The people in Atlanta put it on the line. Rappahannock County could take the food program voluntarily, or the Federals would impose it anyhow. Hungry people had to be fed. It wasn't a very friendly letter. After the hullabaloo subsided — Dancer's Image was disqualified, if you recall, for running with a pain-killing drug in his system—Newbill got around to answering the letter. He said he didn't know of any real hunger in Rappahannock County, and neither did the county health and welfare officials.

Atlanta shot back a hot letter saying that the 1960 Census showed that 51.8 per cent of Rappahannock's families had incomes below $3,000. Newbill responded mildly by saying the figures were deceptive, because practically everyone in Rappahannock has a garden and a few chickens, and some families still raise a few hogs. Besides, said Newbill, getting a little warm himself, jobs were going begging in Rappahannock County. There was plenty of work available for anyone who wanted to raise the median income. Atlanta was not impressed.

The next thing that happened was that one day in June, Jimmy Falls was cutting hay down at the south end of my place, when three men came along in a big black government car. They were coats-and-ties fellows. They obviously were looking for Jimmy. Myrtle Falls or Mr. Burke, or somebody, had told them where to find him. The men hallooed. Jimmy mowed up to the fence line, got down off his tractor, and they

54

all shook hands. It turned out that the men were from the USDA. They had heard that Jimmy knew something about the grocery business; they had come to get a Poverty Program going; and they offered him a contract to run a new food distribution center three days a month.

Jimmy thought it over for a while. He didn't want to make a snap decision. If anyone ever organized a Hard Work Party, with a motto of Stand On Your Own Two Feet, Jimmy Falls would be its national chairman. Jimmy Falls is not what you would call soft on welfare. But he finally agreed to serve and a little later the men from USDA hired Garfield Burke to serve as Jimmy's assistant.

Meanwhile the Feds rented the old grocery and hardware store on Gay Street in Washington, situated cattywampus from the Courthouse. The store had been vacant for a couple of years — no one ever has been able to run a successful business operation in that place — and the green paint was peeling from the walls and ceiling, but it served the purpose well. The government men sent in a truckload of surplus food, and the Poverty Program was in business.

The Federals were under some misapprehension that our county is composed mostly of black families, the county being so statistically poor. Actually our 1960 population numbered 4,423 white and 945—or about 17.6 per cent—nonwhite. The people from Atlanta sent the word down that a colored person would have to be hired as "eligibility supervisor." This was a key position, demanding considerable skill in computation. Jimmy and Garfield inquired around, but found no takers in the black community. The Feds then scoured the county themselves, and finally came up with old Charlie Lewis. He is held in universally high regard, but no one ever thought of Charlie Lewis in a clerical capacity. He gave the job all he had. The figuring proved too much. He quit on the fifth day. In desperation the USDA sent in a white female bookkeeper to take over. Jimmy and Garfield stuck with the operation. They dutifully handed out dried beans, cornmeal, and twelve other commodities to the 80 or 90 families certified as eligible. One of the regulations was that they had to pass out raisins also. The raisins, sad to say, were not a success. Most of the boxes of raisins reportedly wound up on the Sperryville Dump, on the banks of the Thornton River down near the Farmers' Co-op. There is never much of anything to do for summer recreation in Rappahannock County, and this was a help. People went down to the Sperryville Dump to look at the thrown-away raisins.

The affair didn't actually tear the county asunder, like the hiring of a new game warden or the appointment of a deputy sheriff, but it caused some heated conversations. One faction took the view that as long as the government was *giving* food away, Rappahannock would be foolish not to get in on the act. An opposing faction argued that such craven expediency was wrong in principle. Well, said the first faction, heating up, you don't object to big farmers getting paid for taking land out of cultivation. That's an entirely different proposition, said the second faction. The talk went on and on.

If it hadn't been for Jimmy Falls and Garfield Burke, the controversy might have gotten ugly, but the Feds knew what they were doing when they stopped that day and talked Jimmy off his tractor. Jimmy teaches Sunday School at the Woodville Baptist Church; he enjoys the rare distinction of being both liked and respected. When Garfield's participation was announced, the Poverty Program's stock went up; everyone agreed that nobody named Burke would be in this thing if it weren't all right.

After a while, I forget when, it all petered out. The program expired, or the food ran out, or food stamps came on the scene. One day we looked around and the store was empty again. The poor folks, plenty puzzled, went back to being poor. The Sperryville Dump lost its prime attraction. By the spring of 1969, when Willie Hartack won his fifth Derby on Majestic Prince, we had our priorities straight and were back to talking horses again.

In a rural county as small as ours, it's said that "everyone knows everyone else." It isn't true, of course, for Virginians as a breed put great store in privacy and in the right to be let alone. Even so, people know generally about other people — who's adding on to his house, who lost a cow, who got a deer on Opening Day, who's bought a new pickup truck or tractor — and the sense of community has considerable meaning. Thus, when death comes to one of our leading families, the death is widely and instantly felt. But there is something about country living: The fact of death is just as instantly accepted.

Garfield Burke died of a Tuesday late in June of 1971. He was buried on Thursday in the little graveyard at Woodville. The Reverend B. Gayle Titchenell, who delivered the eulogy, touched on the universal question that forever arises: *Why Garfield?* He was only 38, a young husband and father. Until cancer felled him, he seemed in perfect health—strong, wiry, a clear-eyed farmer who could make hay for 12 hours and never get tired. It seemed especially unfair for death to claim Garfield Burke. Mr. Titchenell responded to the unspoken protest by saying, as all preachers do, that we have to understand it was the Lord's will. Such understanding comes hard.

But life goes on. That is the understanding that comes easier. The Burkes had planted 20 acres of the high meadow in corn that summer, and early on the morning after the funeral Garfield's brother-in-law, Jimmy Falls, was up there with the big tractor working the crop. Garfield's father, Weldon Burke, was then our rural letter carrier; later that Friday morning he was back on the road, delivering mail out of Woodville. The Burkes' General Store was open for business as usual. There were cattle that had to be looked after, and gardens that had to be tended, and eggs that had to be gathered. Life goes on.

It may be — I venture the idea tentatively — that country people develop a certain stoicism about death that city dwellers somehow miss. In the midst of our life, we are *always* in death. Most of the farming here is cattle farming, chiefly of Black Angus. The sullen beasts have their doom written in their dark and heavy heads. On some distant and inevitable

57

Thursday, they know the tumbrels await for the auctioneer's call. Country life is geared to living and dying, to the yielding seed, the killing frost, the dead wood that finds a certain resurrection in bright flame and fertile ash. One never has to look far for the carrion birds; they are forever gliding, circling, moseying around, writing charcoal spirals in the sky. The slain deer, the dead calf — dead for no visible reason — are constant parts of our world. We know, without really thinking about it, that chains of life are moving always around us. The chorus of frogs sounds a great amen.

Garfield's death moved me to brood about these things. It was not very original brooding, for keener observers and wiser philosophers have been riding this same train of thought since time began. But the summer of 1971 was a good summer for reflection. It was a big year for fireflies. One week there were none at all; the next week they were out in flickering swarms — more lightning bugs than we had seen before or since, their tiny candles adding sparkle to the starry, iridescent night. A week or so later they were gone. So brief a life! Three weeks of summer. Thirty-eight years. For the firefly or the farmer, these are lifetimes, all one has, and then the phosphorescence stops. The light is there; and now it is not there; but the cycle never ends.

That summer of 1971 was an odd year for living creatures generally. When we first came to Rappahannock in 1966, we were told that snakes and chipmunks had suddenly been everywhere observed. This was how it was again in 1971, and as it turned out, again in 1976. Do snakes and chipmunks rise and fall together? It seems a fair surmise. Is some five-year cycle in effect? Perhaps. Twice that summer we came across black snakes somnolent, engorged with chipmunk victims. Lorenzo the collie killed the snakes, snapping their spines in a whiplash toss. We dug a hole in the vegetable garden, buried snakes and chipmunks, and down in the dark earth the worms and funeral beetles went to work. Life goes on.

It was an unusually wet summer also, and this meant great nights for the night hunters. It is useless to turn out the hounds when the countryside is hot and dry, but rainy seasons are something else. Scent rises from the fields and the damp forest floors, and by 11 o'clock every evening you can hear the hounds in cry. These are small hounds, lean and purposeful as marathon runners; they stream across the hills, intent upon the tasks that hounds are bred for, fox or 'coon, the hunters and the hunted, wagging tails and lolling tongues; and in some stubbled rocky field you find the visceral remains of their prey. These are among the patterns by which our lives are tailored, tonight the gibbous moon, tomorrow the full; it all goes on.

Men, birds, animals, insects — my not very novel thought is that the marvel and the mystery lie in the infinite rotations. It is the same with plants. The summer of Garfield's death, owing largely to the recurring rains, was a time of prodigal growth. Our roadsides were a forest of day lilies, red as old barns; of blue chicory, massed honeysuckle, black-eyed susans, daisies that might have been lacquered in bone-white enamel. The dill leaped to spectacular heights, the slim stems shooting up like roman candles to explode in yellow diadems. The weeds grew as lushly as well. Nothing could be contained. But after the summer came October's frost; and the frost killed, as they say; and everything died, or so it seemed. It all rotted, leaves and weeds and lilies, and so the rotation resumed. They buried Garfield Burke in the Woodville graveyard. I cannot believe the rotation leaves out men.

If I have left the impression that there's nothing much to do in Rappahannock County, socially speaking, the impression ought to be corrected. Friends get together for all kinds of reasons. They go to church meetings in the winter and to revivals in the summer. There's a tennis tournament every Labor Day. October is apple butter time. And in November a few old-timers still kill hogs.

There was a time when almost every household in Rappahannock raised a few hogs for home consumption. Those days are just about gone. Pigs are mean-tempered beasts, shifty-eyed and sly; they have an air about them; raising them is more trouble than you might think. In the old days there were plenty of small butcher shops that would help with the slaughtering process, but most of those were done in by the antiseptic requirements of Federal regulations. Hog slaughter, country style, is getting to be a lost art. I am minded to record such an event for a society that may suppose pork chops are born from glassine wombs and laid in supermarket cribs.

On the Monday after Thanksgiving a couple of years ago, Tommy and Dorothy Taylor, with sons Tom and Bill, spent the day in the hog killing process. The Taylors had only two hogs of their own, but Paul Alther had a few, and somebody's aunt had a couple, and by the time the sun came up that Monday morning a dozen pigs were in prospect.

If you had been along, you would have climbed into a pickup truck about 7:30, and rattled off to Redaviva and Smedley, down the twisting road that lies below Pickerel Ridge, around a couple of other mountains and back again. It was bitterly cold, the sky the color of newsprint, ice on the ponds. We finally stopped by an old barn, walked across a frozen field, past a turnip patch and a woodpile, crushing broom sedge under foot, and there was the pigpen.

Tom and Bill and their father, with Paul Alther, climbed over the fence. The two black hogs were waiting, swaying sullenly on their oddly dainty feet, wary and suspicious. Bill knelt, leveling a .22 rifle with a countryman's confident ease, and shot the first hog squarely between the eyes. Paul Alther leaped forward with a knife and made one quick clean cut. The second hog followed the first, and it was over in a matter of seconds. They dragged the two hogs across the field, heaved them into the truck, and we rattled back to the Taylors' place.

The Taylors live close to the North Fork of the Thornton River. Down on the riverbank, just upstream from Piney Run, they had dug a trench maybe two feet wide and two feet deep and six feet long. Well before dawn the sons had filled the

60

trench with firewood and put a great iron tub of river water on to boil. By the time we returned with the first two hogs, it was 8 o'clock and the water was bubbling. Each of the hogs weighed over 250 pounds, and they seemed to have gotten heavier in death. The Taylor boys hooked a chain around the hind legs, and with a good deal of heaving and grunting, hoisted them one by one to the tub.

There Lee Fincham took charge. He is a tall leathery man, who was turned out that morning in work shirt, old sweater, and a bright red hunting cap. We have lots of Finchams in this part of the Blue Ridge country. Out of curiosity, I just counted the Finchams in the phone book: fifty-three, and it's a small phone book. Lee Fincham is the brother of Sleepy Fincham, who used to look after grounds and buildings at the old high school in Washington before they built the new school down near Sperryville. Every boy and girl who ever went to the old school knew him. Now Sleepy Fincham does some house painting and a little of everything else.

I mentioned Paul Alther. He's a cousin of Johnny Alther, whose wife Hilda Alther is our cleaning woman. She comes on Wednesdays and Fridays, and she never stops working. Hilda is a sturdy countrywoman, silent but cheerful; she rarely says more than half a dozen words at a time, but there's contentment in her face. It's important for you to know these people.

Anyhow, the hogs were lifted by the chain hoist one at a time and plunked into the boiling water. After a few minutes of scalding, they were rolled onto a scraping table. Bristle scraping is a specialized art. Lee Fincham used nothing but his gnarled red hands. Paul Alther preferred the sharp zinc top off an old Mason jar. The Taylors used knives. After 15 minutes of dipping, scalding and scraping, a hog was scraped down to his clean white skin. The carcass then was suspended from a tripod gantry, and Lee Fincham did the gutting. The Taylor boys brought buckets of water from the river and washed the carcass till their hands were freezing. Thin rivulets of blood trickled down to the river and formed a red fringe at the icy edges. A gallery of five country dogs sniffed happily around the steaming entrails. The process took all morning.

That was only the beginning for the Taylor family. Monday evening Dorothy and the two girls, Susan and C.C., got into the production line. They cut and salted the hams and shoulders. Tuesday and Wednesday they worked on sausage. By Thursday night they were through with the lard—the lard to season country biscuits all winter long. The Althers and the Finchams, in their own kitchens, were doing the same thing. Everybody's cure is just a little different; nobody's sausage tastes exactly like another's. Probably it's only imagination working, but a hog that is scalded over an oak and hickory fire, and washed clean in icy water from the North Fork of the Thornton River, somehow makes better bacon than a hog that is slaughtered in the city. Anyhow, we like to think so.

Not all our local characters are local characters. Some of our local characters are imported from the Great Beyond. One such character is Tom Geoghegan. He invents.

This is not his full-time occupation, to be sure. Professionally speaking, my brother Geoghegan is Washington news director for U. S. Steel. He is short and white-haired and rising 60 as this is written in 1977. His good eye — his right eye — stays alight with amazement. He has the general bearing of a leprechaun, size medium-large. He swears by a single-minded devotion to the ultimate pot of gold.

The Geoghegans and the Kilpatricks met on a junket to Greece in 1971. Tom had just invented a microscopic gyroscope, too small for the human eye to see, guaranteed to keep airplanes safely in the air. This he had cleverly sewed into the brim of Martha's hat, Martha being his patient but terrified wife. Thus equipped, Martha flew a DC-10 to Athens and back again. The plane never bumped, shuddered, or rolled over. A pleasanter flight could not be imagined.

One thing led to another, and two years later Tom bought 25 beautiful acres of Rappahannock, just across the road from White Walnut Hill. There he set about the business of planting apple trees, and after a two-year interruption for a heart attack, set about building a house. The first room to be constructed, naturally enough, was an inventing room just off the garage.

At one time he had planned simply to move up the dog-house from his home in Chevy Chase, and to use that for inventing. After the movers gave him an estimate, he abandoned the thought. It doubtless is a risky business to say that Geoghegan's doghouse is the most impressive doghouse east of the Mississippi, for superlatives get you into trouble. But certainly there can be few doghouses in its class.

This was a structure erected for a Great Dane who could put her front paws, when she wanted to show off, on the top of a seven-foot door jamb. They named her Czarnie, which is Polish for "Blacky." Don't ask me why. Tom started to build a modest, ordinary, perfectly conventional house for her, but the project — as Tom's projects tend to do — got swiftly out of hand. Before he was finished, the edifice had pegged floors, a Dutch door, a bay window, two other windows, a shingled roof, a gable, and a cupola on top. It had wall to wall carpeting, two electric receptacles, a stereo system, a framed photograph of Gielgud playing Hamlet, and a six-foot flagpole from which the red and white flag of Denmark could on ceremonial occasions be bravely flown.

Halfway through the construction project, Tom wired a broom to the top steel beam and threw a topping-out party. When the work was finally done, we had a Dedication Day complete with Press Releases. "Ten thousand pounds of steel nails were required for the Great Danish Manor House, T. Geoghegan, chief supervisor of the massive work, disclosed today. If laid end to end, the nails would stretch for 1,100 miles . . ." And so on.

The only problem that developed — a problem of no signifi-cance — was that when the house was done, Czarnie refused to sleep in it. Czarnie (pronounced Charney) slept on a dis-carded twin bed mattress in the garage. Tom thought about furnishing the doghouse with a queen-sized bed, a dresser and a rocker, and using the place for guests, but converted it to a woodworking shop instead. This was his inventing room, and he used to sit there gazing out the bay window onto the patio beyond and reflecting on ways to make a million.

One day his lucubrations were interrupted by a neighbor, Margaret Hemenway, who rang the door chimes of Czarnie's Manor House looking for Martha, and found the sage alone. In the course of casual conversation it developed that Mrs. Hemenway recently had seen a TV program known as "Hollywood Squares." An expert guest on the program, if I have my facts straight, had been asked if the yield of a fruit tree could be improved by swatting the tree on the trunk. However improbable it may sound, the expert's answer was yes.

This remarkable advice caught my brother Geoghegan just at the start of his great apple tree period. Sparks flew from his inventive mind. His good eye rolled. His hair stood on end. Struck by inspiration, he leaped to the telephone to let me know that at last our fortunes were about to be made. We would forthwith form a corporation, he explained, to develop and market a product that would burst like hoola-hoops upon a breathlessly expectant world. Because he liked me, and wanted to see a young fellow get ahead, he would let me put up all the working capital and have a small share of the stock. He would be president of the corporation, of course, and would serve also as vice president for public relations.

The corporation was to be called Trunk Thunkers, Inc., and what we would make, if you had been wondering, was the first implement designed especially and particularly, though not necessarily exclusively, for the thunking of trunks.

Well, we were carried away. President Geoghegan embraced his duties in the serene conviction that Americans will buy anything — absolutely anything — if only they are approached in the proper way. This was several years before the Christmas of the Pet Rock, which clearly proved his theory. Tom's thought was to approach American consumers in a few improper ways as well.

"The first appeal," said our president, "will be to the tree owner's sense of guilt. 'Are you giving your trees the care they're entitled to have?' After a few months, every American who isn't thunking his trunks will feel he's neglecting his children. Then we appeal to the success ethic: 'Is your pet fig an underachiever? Is it living up to its full potential?'"

Geoghegan charted a regional campaign to appeal to the industrious New Englander: "Are your maples lazy? Loafing on you? A few hearty licks with our Model W-4000 Trunk Thunker will have them producing in no time." He talked of lining up a white-coated professor, Dr. J. Sebastian Barck, the noted arborist, to handle our TV commercials. The endorsement of a titled Englishman, he figured, would add a certain class. That was how he invented Lord Clivedon of Clove (or was it Lord Cloveden of Clive?), the well-known owner of Sherwood Forest, who thunked his every trunk with a Model W-4000. He engaged his daughter, a ravishing beauty by the name of Sheila, to pose for photographs suggesting that a suburban housewife could thunk one-handedly. The campaign would have made advertising history.

As for the thunker itself, we envisioned a solid plastic core, swathed in Styrofoam in the customer's choice of decorator colors, that could be marketed in a simulated leather carrying case for $9.95. Please indicate for left or right hand. There would be a full selection of sizes and weights, but there would be no economy model. Only DeLuxe and Super DeLuxe. Our sales managers would be instructed to suggest the versatility of this indispensable whopper: When not being put to its intended use in orchard or grove, our product would crush ice, smash pecans, drive nails, or quiet noisy children; it would roll dough, stop a door or a bill collector, prop up a window, or, depending upon the model, serve as bung starter, sand wedge or fungo bat. We estimated our profit at $9.90 each, an earnings rate surpassed only by that of a good tax accountant.

Alas, nothing ever came of Trunk Thunkers, Inc., but the idea was essentially sound. The idea was to mass-produce a product that no one needs and to sell it at a price no patriotic fellow could refuse. In any event, if the product didn't take hold, we could have sold our company's motto neatly framed: THUNK!

Our empire crumbled before it even got half-baked. Someone else, if you will believe it, came up with the identical product and actually marketed the thing under the trademarked name of Encounterbat. It was a device for venting one's hostilities. In 1976 the product was regularly advertised in such high-toned magazines as *Human Behavior* and *Psychology Today:* "Warning — Bottled-up Aggression is Dangerous to Your Health." That was the way their ads began. The Encounterbat offered "the satisfying and fun way to pound out pent-up emotions." Their bats were made from sturdy, durable foam, 6 inches in diameter and 24 inches long, which was a little longer than we had figured, and they had a handle that could be gripped with both hands. The bats were overpriced, I thought, at $23.63 a pair, but who am I to knock a nice profit? In a spirit of scientific inquiry, I bought a couple of the things, marched over to Tom's growing apple orchard, and gave the number one tree a wallop that would have felled a Missouri mule. It didn't do a damned thing for the tree, but it left me in good spirits the rest of the day.

In talking a little while ago about the recreational attractions of Rappahannock County, I mentioned church socials and hog killings, but I forgot to mention a big one: baseball. Except for an occasional polo match at Bill Fannon's place, baseball is the only spectator sport we have. Our high school, small as it is, annually fields one of the finest high school teams in northern Virginia. At Castleton, a few miles from Scrabble, Homer Henry built two beautiful diamonds and a grandstand just for the pure pleasure of slow pitch softball. Teams come from as far as York, Pennsylvania, to play in his slow pitch tournaments. On a warm Saturday in summer, 1,200 spectators turn out to watch the confrontations of such athletic aggregations as the Rental Uniform Service of Culpeper, the White House Realty Company of Fairfax, and Al's Sporting Goods of Fredericksburg.

Slow pitch, which offers seven-inning games with ten on a side, is a far cry from major league ball, but if you are a baseball nut you will watch anything — Little League, high school, sandlot, slow pitch, anything. An addiction to baseball knows no cure.

My own love affair with baseball goes back to Oklahoma City in the 1920's. My father was in the lumber business, selling fence posts, railway ties and bridge flooring. When a civic movement developed for a new ballpark, down by the reservoir, he contributed some of the heavy timber for the grandstand and wound up with a lifetime pass to a box behind the Indians' dugout. Every summer afternoon, when the Indians were at home, he took me out to the ballgame. Over a period of seven or eight years, until I got a summer job as a copyboy for the *Oklahoma City Times,* I don't believe we missed a one.

On game days I used to take the streetcar downtown to his office in the old Insurance Building on Broadway. He had an adding machine that operated with a hand crank, like a one-armed bandit, a delightful contraption. He had a rack of rubber stamps. I used to practice typing on a venerable Remington that must have dated from the Civil War. There were plenty of things to help a boy fidget his time away.

Finally Father would sign the last of his mail, put on his coat, fix his panama hat firmly on his massive head, and we would drive majestically out to the ballgame. He was an impressive figure of a man—a great brow, bushy eyebrows, large nose, luxurious mustache, solid jaw. He looked more like a judge than a lumberman. As I recall, he had his own privileged parking space — it came with the lifetime pass — where the Nash sedan could repose in state. Going up the grandstand ramp with Father was like climbing Olympus with God.

Under his grave tutelage, I began to learn some of the subtleties and nuances of this most ingenious and demanding game—the pitchout, the change-up, the intentional walk, the ballet movements of an infield, the meaning of a perfect bunt and a sacrifice fly. Father used to keep score with a slim gold Eversharp pencil — why would I remember that after all these years? — and he had his own mark for an error. It was a large E in a black box. When he rendered the dreadful judgment, it was a symbol of doom itself. He was never given to shouting encouragement — he was much too dignified for that—but he had his own way of demonstrating unrestrained approval: He would clap three times: clap, clap, clap. When an Indian hit a home run, Father would invariably stand. Maybe he wasn't the typical fan, but he was a steady one.

Father knew the ticket takers, ushers, players, managers, and club owners. When I was 10 or 11, I badgered him into getting me a tryout as bat boy. He used his influence, and sure enough, one afternoon I got myself to the ballpark an hour ahead of time, donned a uniform not much too big and baggy, and set about a bat boy's chores. It was very nearly a disaster. Let me be painfully honest: It was a disaster. I was so mesmerized, so absolutely enchanted, so dazed by the glorious moment that I walked as in a dream between the pitcher and catcher, warming up along the first base foul line. The pitcher's fast ball hummed like a hornet past my ear, not a quarter-inch away. I can feel the 90-mile-an-hour wind of that nearly fatal missile to this day. The shaken pitcher, unnerved by the experience, walked the first three men he faced, gave up a triple that cleared the bases, and got jerked before he could get a man out. Stomping from the mound, he sought me out as the source of his woes and gave me a cursing of truly professional polish. It was my first and last day as bat boy.

The shameful incident doubtless moved me to tears, but nothing could lessen the love affair. There were giants in those days. It is true, as Gibbon remarked, that men tend always to exalt the past and to deprecate the present. But verily, it was something special to grow up in the time of Ruth and Gehrig and Foxx. In my nonage in Oklahoma City, we were mostly Cardinal fans. Our heroes were Ducky Medwick and John Mize and the Dean brothers. During the 1934 series—I was 13 at the time — we almost expired in exultation.

Baseball then was truly the national pastime. Nothing else touched it. Sure, we kept up with Walter Hagen and later with Gene Sarazen in golf, with Bill Tilden and later Fred Perry in tennis. We hated Max Schmeling and we pitied poor Primo Carnera. High school football was an autumn passion. But baseball for a boy was the be-all and end-all.

Those days, I suppose, are gone. Major league attendance remains at high levels, but because of the disappearance of so many minor leagues, total attendance at professional baseball continues its sad decline. Violence and speed are the new obsessions. Football, basketball, hockey, auto racing — all these seem to have greater appeal.

True, baseball has its times of tedium. There is not much zing in three-up, three-down. A couple of years ago, in this regard, I did a terrible thing. I delivered myself of a television commentary in which I suggested that if the moguls of baseball refused to jazz up the grand old game, baseball would go the way of the blue whale and the whooping crane.

I cannot explain why I said these awful things. Perhaps the commentary resulted from a high fever, left over from a bout of flu. More likely, it was the devil's work. In some inexplicable way, I may have been trying to throw a beanball at my traditionalist, conservative followers in the viewing audience: Keep 'em loose. Don't let them crowd the plate.

In any event, in my madness I actually proposed a gin fizz gimmick: Score two runs, I proposed, instead of one, if a runner steals home or makes home on a squeeze bunt. George F. Will, my brother conservative, happened to be in the studio when I taped this outrage. He was aghast. "Communist!" he croaked. "Bolshevik!" When I expanded upon the supposed virtues of the squeeze bunt bonus, he fainted dead away and had to be revived with spirits of malt. The following Sunday a sports writer in the Washington *Post* gave me a public hiding I richly deserved. Now, George Will is a baseball nut. He is nuttier than I am. He does not adorn his study, as the rest of us do, with paintings of Genghis Khan, Edmund

Burke, and John C. Calhoun. He tends toward framed photographs of Ernie Banks. George is a Cubs nut. He has to be crazy. In 1976 he gave himself a Christmas present: He invested $542, or some such sum, in one share of stock in the Chicago Cubs. This was just three months after his hapless warriors finished in fourth place in the Eastern Division, with a won-lost record of 75-87, a tidy 26 games out of first place. Greater faith has no investor ever shown.

Various metaphysicians have had a go at explaining baseball's allure. One fellow, a closet astrologist, had a theory that involved the mystic number of three: three outs, three strikes, three outfielders, 60 feet between home plate and the pitcher's mound, 90 feet between the bases, a 90-degree quadrant for the playing field itself. Another philosopher credited a large part of the game's attraction to the massive body of comparative statistics accumulated over the past hundred years. Still another scholar has remarked baseball's contributions to the language. People are forever using the verb, usually incorrectly, to *pinch hit.* By metaphorical extension, *foul ball, curve ball, change-up, pop-up, stolen base,* and *double play,* have enlarged our vocabulary.

My own theory (I'm sure others have propounded it also) is that we love baseball because it is the only one of our major team sports that has no time limitation. Football, basketball, hockey — even rugby and soccer and polo — have their fixed terminations. When the clock grinds down to 00:00, that's it. But a baseball game, in theory, could go on like the Pottstown Piping Band; it could go on forever; it might never be concluded. In a society bedeviled by deadlines — by airline schedules that must be met, by eight-hour shifts and 30-minute lunch breaks, by 60-second commercials — baseball offers a measure of surcease. We are too much ruled by reins that are held by hour and minute hands. We are choked by high-speed action, hot lines, instant replays, microwave biscuits, direct dial phones and satellite relays.

Thus surfeited, we go out to the ballgame. The pitcher is unhurried; he paws the mound, rubs the ball, hitches his pants, adjusts his cap, spits three times, examines the sky, the infield, the outfield, and the opposing hitter. Then he asks the umpire for a fresh ball, and massages that one for a while. After every put-out come the ritual pepper throws. With two out and a base empty, we get the intentional walk. The batter might more expeditiously be waved to first base, but no: Four careful pitch-outs are required. It was a blow to the game when reformers began to provide golf carts to speed a reliefer in from the bullpen. The long, slow amble was better. Baseball ought never to be hurried. It is the only unhurried institution we have left, which is one reason, I think, that we love it.

Maybe love will sustain the game forever. Other sports may arouse wilder passions than baseball, but none kindles more enduring affection. And baseball is not without its passions, either. When we were living in Richmond, my pint-sized wife had a crush on an umpire by the name of Augie Gugielmo. The Italian vibes were working. He used to call strikes with the magisterial grace of a traffic cop in Florence. A great umpire. But he had had a bad night, and the fans at Parker Field were giving him a terrible time. Inning after inning, they jeered and booed. Robber! Blind Tom! In the bottom half of the eighth, when he called one of our heroes out on a doubtful strike, the stands erupted more wildly than before.

After a moment, one of those sudden silences fell, to be broken in astonishing fashion. It was broken by my lovely, mannered, convent-educated bride, who drew herself up, five feet and 90 pounds of fury, and cupped her hands around her trembling lips to cry at the offending grandstand: "Get off Augie's back, you lousy bums!" Out on the field, in back of home plate, Gugielmo visibly quivered. Then he shook with laughter. The fickle fans turned to cheering, and when the inning ended Augie strutted in our direction—not to bow, or give a wave of thanks, or anything so fearfully unseemly, but just to treat one adoring fan to his splendid profile.

The magic abides—the crack of bat, the flight of ball, the runners moving, the suspense of the lonely duel between pitcher and batter with men on base. This is the stuff of which

Camelot was made — skills, and nerve, and grace afield, and sweet dreams of pennants rippling out in centerfield. Here in Rappahannock County, we go over to Homer Henry's place to watch the Castleton Kings, or down to Amissville to root for the Early Birds who play for the Early Carpet Company. It falls short of watching the Reds or the Yankees, but who cares? A really bad ballgame will never on this earth be played.

Almost every household, I suppose, has its little store of adages that fall into common use — the ounce of prevention that is worth a pound of cure, the stitch in time that saves nine, the reminder that tomorrow is another day. Into every life some rain must fall. This too will pass.

These apothegms serve a purpose: They lubricate the bearings of everyday life; they ease the frictions of existence. At White Walnut Hill we fell long ago into a recurring phrase that reassures: *That's country living.* Have mice built a nest in a fur-lined boot? That's country living. Is there a black snake in the rafters of the tool shed? That's country living. Has the tractor broken down? The pump lost its prime? Is there a footloose cow in the middle of the road? Is that poison ivy on your arm? Country living.

Some of the time, I confess, we do tend to think of country living only in terms of inconvenience. The differences between country life and city life are immensely varied. Some of the shortcomings of rural existence are immediately apparent. One cannot attend a ballet at Flint Hill, or see a play at Sperryville, or saunter through the great museums of Scrabble. There's no French restaurant in Peola Mills. Prices are high at the stores, and the choice of goods is severely curtailed.

In the whole of Rappahannock County there is not a bowling alley, a golf course, a pool hall, a delicatessen, a liquor store, a bookstore, or a place to get a TV set repaired. There's not even a drive-in movie; the last one, over near Massie's Corner, closed a few years ago. Law enforcement is rudimentary; the public schools are not that hot; public health services are minimal, and everyone takes his own non-burnable trash to a county dump. The burnable trash, of course, you burn yourself. There's no hospital. The fire department, of which we are truly proud, is wholly volunteer. We have three doctors, two of them part-time and one who is mostly retired. No dentist. We don't even have a veterinarian since Bill Wake retired. One barber shop. One beauty shop. No funeral home. No McDonalds, Burger Kings, or Tastee Freezes. No drug store, no pharmacist. I could go on. Within Rappahannock you cannot get a picture framed, or a pair of shoes half-soled, or a tennis racket strung, or a clock repaired. This is country living.

Only one problem is seriously troubling. It truly is no fun to be awakened on a winter night not by the cold, but by the silence. Even in the quietest household, one senses the faint, inaudible hum of refrigerator, freezer, electric clock. Things go click. Thermostats crack their knuckles. But when the power fails, one hears only the redoubtable tick-tock of Grandmother's clock. A futile snapping of the switch on the bedside lamp confirms the inescapable verdict: The kitchen clock is the only mechanism still working. The power is off.

It is true of power outages everywhere, of course, but it is singularly true in the country: When the power goes, every-thing goes. This includes the water pump. City dwellers do not think upon such things. In the country, no power means no water for coffee, no water for shaving or showering, no water to flush the johns. On a winter morning, this means that the husband and head of the household, having first fed the two fireplaces to a roaring blaze, must trek downhill to the spring box, buckets in hand. His exertion is made the more difficult by a helpful collie, whose thought is to lie down directly in front of the husband and head of household, the better to be stepped over. Collies have great senses of humor.

So long as there is plenty of dry firewood at hand, a house built by Arthur Griffith can be kept comfortably warm. A grill can be jerry-rigged in the kitchen fireplace, water can be brought to a boil for coffee. Given a nice bed of embers, bacon and eggs can be fried; they may not truly taste better, but they *seem* to taste better. Nobody starves; the novelty, as I mean to say in a moment, can even be enjoyed; but having no power is a nuisance.

There are compensations—lots of compensations. Country living involves differences in scale, in values, in perspective. Most of the amenities of civilization are not more than 30 to 45 minutes away—an hour and a half at most. Some of the amenities we're just as happy to get along without. In the whole of Rappahannock County, for example, there's not a single traffic light. And if the forces of law and order boil down to Sheriff Buntin, two full-time deputies and one part-time deputy, that's all right. Except for petty thievery and occasional break-ins of the weekenders' vacant cabins, there isn't any crime. We experience perhaps one murder a year, two or three cases of rape a year, and maybe half a dozen cases of aggravated assault. If a Rappahannocker is going to be away from his home for two or three days, of course he locks up; otherwise nobody bothers. I have been sitting here trying to remember when I last heard a voice raised in Rappahannock in really ugly anger, as distinguished from ordinary irritation. I can't remember. In these parts, law violation is largely at the level of throwing beer cans on the shoulder of a road.

You find these compensations all year long. Every summer I try to take a few days off. I cover the old Underwood like a birdcage and forget about the President, the Supreme Court, and Congress. These are times of the seventh-inning stretch.

There is, of course, the usual work to be done around the farm, but such work is work only if you make your living at it. When one is not compelled to ride a tractor, riding a tractor is almost as pleasant as floating around a millpond fishing from a rowboat. Mowing requires no intellectual effort; it demands just enough active thought to miss the rocks and to avoid a kildee's nest. Whether one is making hay or merely cutting grass, the labor is rewarding; the smell of the orchard grass is sweet and clean, the sweat is honest sweat, and the task has a visible terminal point: There's always one last row, and the job is done. At least it is done until the next time.

You talk about values. One afternoon a couple of years ago, over at Hawthorn Farm, son Sean and Billy Nicholson and Allen Smith were getting in wheat. Their rickety old combine dropped a part or threw a shoe, and hours were lost while the men searched vainly for the missing piece. Then a thunderstorm came rolling over Jobbers Mountain, purple as a bruise, and laid the ripe wheat flat. More time was lost while the wheat got back on its feet the next day. They finally patched up the combine and trucked the warm golden grain over to the mill at Rapidan. They got $3.64 a bushel. There wasn't much dollar profit — probably none at all, by strict cost accounting — but there were inner rewards.

The thunderstorm brought fringe benefits. It camped for about five minutes right over our house, and tossed down a couple of scary bolts of lightning. These were close. There was a glare, a zz-a-ap and a crash of thunder all in a single second, and when the dishes stopped rattling the TV sets were dead. This eliminated the morning and evening news, along with the Sunday talk shows, and a man who lives by the news should have felt deprived. It was glorious.

With the media mute, it was possible to watch the barn swallows instead. A pair of them nest in the garage every summer. They build a castle turret of mud, as perfect in its way as the round watch towers of Rhodes, and sometime around Independence Day four or five chicks are hatched. Their fuzzy little black-faced heads hang over the edge of the castle, for all the world like Ollie the Dragon in the old puppet shows. You can pass a solid hour — no trouble at all — watching mama and papa swooping in and out, punching food down those gaping mouths. Swallows are natural-born fighter pilots. They are aerial acrobats who fly for the pure love of flying — barrel rolls, outside loops, Immelmann turns. They will buzz a collie for the sheer unmitigated fun of the thing. And if you want to watch a tender experience, watch a pair of swallows teaching their young to fly. This is the process of discovery, and it never stops. In the summer of 1974 we acquired a buff collie puppy, name of Bagpiper, to provide an heir apparent for the middle-aged Lorenzo. Every day was a day of discovery for Piper. He discovered fledgling quail, and wondered why they fled his romping friendship. He discovered the herb garden, and emerged smelling of thyme, oregano, and sage. He discovered a garter snake, which broadened his education and enlarged his wisdom: Life is not all a bed of oregano. Lorenzo, after a week of jealous sulking, philosophically accepted his tutelary duties. He began to devote his mornings to giving Piper classroom instruction, from 8 to 9 in Rising Majestically, from 9 to 10 in Posing Regally, and from 10 to 12 a lab course in Getting in the Way.

In another summer hiatus, a year later, civic duty called. We drove into little Washington for a hearing before the Board of Zoning Appeals. It was a summer morning suitable for framing: soft sky, cool breeze, the ditch banks alive with chipmunks and rabbits. The chicory, one of our prettiest wild flowers, was in bloom; the flowers were as blue as a granddaughter's eyes.

We took the Shade Road. Six months earlier it would have qualified as one of the loveliest country lanes in this part of Virginia. Then, without notice, warning or reason, crews from the highway department appeared. They revved up their power saws, splintering the winter silence, and cut down a hundred trees. These were great towering oaks and maples, some of them three feet across at the stump. A few months earlier they had formed a Gothic arch across the road. In autumn, driving the Shade Road was like driving through the Cathedral of Notre Dame. Some of the trees were there when young George Washington rode that way.

All this was done, mind you, in the Holy Name of Progress, as part of a widening project. The vandals disappeared as abruptly as they had come, leaving an ugliness behind. But on this morning in July, six months later, we made a discovery. The amputated trees would not give up. They were putting out impertinent new growth. Vines had grown around the stumps. Wild flowers, irrepressible, had reappeared. The raw wounds were healing. So it is, one reflects, with human scars as well: In time the broken heart is honeysuckled over.

Our Courthouse is old red brick, half-columned in white, resting comfortably in a grove of oaks. Outside are a couple of green sitting benches. On down the lawn is a small obelisk honoring the Confederate troops who served from Rappahannock County. Almost every crossroads in Virginia, east of the Shenandoah Valley, is knee-deep in history. If history could be exported like ham or tobacco, Virginia would enjoy a massive trade balance. History is what we have the most of. You cannot go ten miles in Virginia without getting stuck in it. But Rappahannock, regrettably, offers a poor crop. We were nothing much in colonial times; we just missed a chance at glory in the Revolution; and we were always on the fringes of the War for Southern Independence. That was what Dr. Douglas Southall Freeman called it. Mosby's Raiders operated in and out of Rappahannock, but except for a few cavalry skirmishes, that was it. The action was someplace else. That's the story of Rappahannock. The action, praise be, is always somewhere else.

Inside the Courthouse, up a flight of worn stairs, is the courtroom itself: a small bench for our district judge, flags of the State and Nation, a dozen wicker chairs for a jury on the rare occasions when one is actually empaneled. There's a long table, ink-stained, for the lawyers; a slant-top desk for the clerk. Big windows let in great shafts of sunlight, lightly flecked with golden motes. *This is where our law lives.* Looking around that summer morning, I wondered: Is it any less important, so far as our own people are concerned, than the Supreme Court's marble temple? This is all the average Rappahannocker will ever see of the Rule of Law.

On this particular Tuesday the Board of Zoning Appeals was hearing an application for a recreational area. The owners of the land proposed to develop their site for intensive public use: Several hundred "campers" would be coming in. Fifty neighboring owners were on hand to object. They complained of prospective traffic, ensuing litter, the possible pollution of

77

streams. The petitioning property owners responded plaintively that if they were denied a permit for recreational use, there was nothing much they could do to earn an investment on their steep and wooded land.

The dispute evoked ancient issues. We sat in a country courtroom on a summer morning, with a squirrel in an oak tree looking on, and thought of Locke and Burke and Montesquieu, and wise old George Mason. What do we mean by the right to pursue happiness? Is there a right to pursue one's happiness at the expense of one's neighbors? All our farms have fences; we know where the boundaries are. What is the outer limit of liberty? What are the metes that bound our freedom? The street in front of the Courthouse was laid out by Washington in 1749. Philosophically, that summer morning, we were right back at his bench marks. The Board, incidentally, killed the applicants' petition for a zoning change.

Winter has its compensations too. When snow comes to Rappahannock, country living takes on a new dimension. A Southerner embarks with diffidence upon tales of winter tribulations. A decent respect must be paid to those who have too much snow, or never quite enough. This is the way it is with mixed blessings. Poets may rhapsodize over honeysuckle and water hyacinths, but if you farm in the lowlands or live by the bayous, you rapidly lose enthusiasm for them. So it is with snow. A good part of the nation views a foot of fresh snow as Alabama views a field of fire ants. At the same time, one has to sorrow for those transplanted New Englanders, living in palmy exile in Miami or Fort Lauderdale, who hunger for the stuff that Minnesota would gladly give away.

Virginians never know quite what to make of snow. They are like barnyard geese. I read somewhere that a biologist once rated wild geese as having the greatest memories of any creatures known to science; barnyard geese, by contrast, evidently think the world begins anew each day. They cannot remember what happened yesterday afternoon. That is how it is with

Virginians and snow. In Brainerd or Fargo or Butte, a couple of inches of snow can fall before breakfast, and nobody looks up from his flapjacks. The same snow in Virginia is a major event. The Richmond papers break out their 96-point Second Coming type: "Blizzard Paralyzes City." All the schools close; a thousand cars slide into a thousand other cars; we suffer something awful. Truth is, we ordinarily suffer mighty little.

I remember our first snow at White Walnut Hill. It began falling on a Monday night early in February, 1967. The same snow in Grand Island, Nebraska, would have been a mere flurry. In the end, it amounted to not more than eight or ten inches — an ordinary snow, quite undistinguished — but it was the sort of snow that every man ought to experience, literally or metaphorically, a couple of times every year.

Earlier in the day I had been working around the place with Charlie Settle and his stepson Richard, building a stone retaining wall. More accurately, Charlie and Richard were doing the work and I was serving as consultant. This is a fine arrangement. But after a while it got too cold to work, and we went over near Sperryville, down the F. T. Valley Road toward Madison, to see a man about a split-rail fence, but he had gone to the store and wouldn't be back till dark. We quit for the day.

Driving home, I nodded at the dark and swollen skies. We were in for a bad one, I said. This was the natural pessimism of the city boy. It is not true that countrymen are by nature pessimistic, and city folk the opposite. Quite the reverse is true. The city man always expects the worst — smog, crime, corruption, tensions on the job, ceilings that leak, noisy neighbors. The countryman, poor devil, has to be an optimist; he has to live in the unwavering hope that his chickens will lay, the hay will make, and the price on hogs will go up. If the farmer ever fell to speculating upon the multiple conspiracies that beset him — the rocky soil, the fickle rain, the distant markets, the whole business of buying at retail and selling at wholesale — the farmer would fall into melancholia and never turn a spade. I digress.

"No, indeed," said Charlie. "The wust of this winter is past."

He had seen a flock of kildees on a hill; a neighbor had killed a snake the week before; crocus shoots were up; the dogwoods were swelling. It might snow a little, he allowed, but it wouldn't amount to much.

The first flakes fell at 7 o'clock. Coming in from the woodpile, I felt the cold wet kiss of snow. In an instant, or so it seemed, the night had become a magic theater and the hemlocks a corps de ballet. A big spruce was hoopskirted and ruffled, a small pine in tutu. Yet the moment was caught on a soundless stage. Living in the city, we forget what silence is. In the whole of the night, only the snow was moving, falling, falling straight down, straight as lace curtains; sifting, clinging, obscuring the ruts of the red clay road. This was the way it was while Snow White slept, with the woods in ermine and the world enchanted.

At dawn the snow was falling still, and all the world was white on white, the fallen trees embossed upon the hill, the new stone wall a perfect parapet. The Rudasill's Mill Road had vanished as completely as if an illusionist had waved his wand. There was only a white cotton blanket spread in a split-rail crib. When at last the snow stopped, it left behind a wedding cake morning, the trees with pearl embroidered trains, edged in frosted lace. From the kitchen window of the cottage, we could see only the birds in intermittent flight—red cardinals and blue juncos, titmice and grosbeaks, a ragged band of urchin sparrows.

All that morning the radio crackled of meetings cancelled, of schools closed, of speeches postponed, of stores and factories shutting down. Charlie telephoned to report a total immobility at Woodville. It is a condition not altogether unknown when the sun is shining.

Abruptly the thought struck home: We were snowed in. Ordinarily any one of three roads will take us out to what, provisionally, may be styled as civilization. You can go south to Woodville, or north to Sperryville, or east by way of the Shade Road and come out on Route 211 just past the high school. We telephoned around the neighborhood. It would be pointless, it appeared, even to try to clear the driveway, for the Woodville road was blocked by 12-foot drifts on down by Clifton Clark's place. The Sperryville road was blocked at Jim Bill Fletcher's. And the Shade Road was impassable also.

These advisories produced a twinge of panic, and the mind probes at panic like a tongue at a toothache. If there were a fire, the volunteers couldn't get through. If there were a serious accident — a heart attack, a broken bone — no rescue squad could be summoned. Eventually, we figured, someone would come to dig us out. Jimmy Falls would plow around the Woodville drift, in order to get hay to his cattle. Mr. Manwaring would send Bob Grigsby to rediscover the driveway. Highway crews in time would do the rest. Meanwhile, we were prisoners.

Then a second thought struck home: Accept it. The thought has recurred many times since. In the sum total of man's brief span upon the earth, what would be missed? Truly missed? So the choirboys would not rehearse, nor the Kiwanians convene that day, and the schoolboys of Culpeper would miss the conjugation of their verbs. For the time being, there could be no further work upon the new stone wall; but the wall could wait. Somewhere a local court had closed; but justice would be done tomorrow, or the day after, or next week.

It is no bad thing, for a while at least, to find oneself snowbound. In his poignant novel of World War I, *The Fountain,* Lewis Morgan put this feeling of cessation into words. In winter, he wrote, time stands still; nothing changes so long as snow is on the ground. And when time stands still, there is time for those things one never has time for otherwise. There are books to be read, and nuts to be cracked, and stamps to be put in philatelic albums. Most especially, there is time to talk. We do so little of that these days, for there are always Things That Have To Be Done; there are always appointments that must be kept, and deadlines that must be met. We get absorbed in the getting and spending.

Snowbound, it is possible to get absorbed in the things that count, in the giving and sharing of love that glows with a steady lantern's light, in the easy communion of books and conversation. There is a certain freedom in captivity, a certain peacefulness in being prisoner. In the mountains, the absolute obligations come down to very few—to feed the animals, to keep the fires going, to look after the elementary necessities of existence. It is wonderful to discover how many things, without calamity, can be postponed. Too soon the snowplow comes, a great orange beetle, grossly beaked, grinding a path by which schoolboys and choirs and Kiwanians can meet again. We learn from snowbound days.

All this is wrapped up in "country living." Nothing much happens up here in the Blue Ridge Mountains — only life, birth, death, law, philosophy, the harvest of a summer, the etched impression of a snowy night. That's how it is in Scrabble, a dateline rather less famed than Paris, London, Washington, or New York. It's not what you would call one of the great news centers of the world, but it rests right in the heart of what matters.

Part Three

In which we examine the fauna.
The flora come later.

This is foxhunting country, here on the slopes of the Blue Ridge Mountains. Among some of the gentry it's the main topic of conversation, year in and year out, but once you get south of Richmond and east of Middleburg the talk peters out. Those who hunt to hounds have learned to be wary of discussing their madness with the unenlightened; some stranger who Brakes for Small Animals is sure to start yelling brutality.

Whatever else the steeplechasing sport may be in precincts less humane than our own, it is positively not brutality here. It may do no harm to correct some wrong impressions. On the face of it, there may seem to be something a little one-sided in the thought of one 15-pound fox being pursued by 26 hounds, one huntsman, two masters, two whippers-in, and a field of 40 horses spurred on by 40 riders, especially when the putative object is not to eat the fox, but simply to kill the critter.

The appearances are misleading. Mark Twain once remarked that the safest place in France is halfway between the pistols of two dueling Frenchmen. By the same token, the safest place for a fox in these hills is about 200 yards in front of the Rappahannock hounds.

This is not to disparage the hounds. They are beautiful animals, white and lemon-spotted, superbly disciplined — at least when the hunt is getting underway. They swim like a school of tropical fish around the feet of the huntsman's horse. They are great actors, capable of playing the role of Slavering Beast, and they have a fine sense of humor. What has eliminated brutality, or so it is said, is the union contract — the contract, plus our subterranean housing supply.

It takes a little explaining. Fox hunting in Rappahannock, one is reliably informed, is strictly governed by an agreement between Local 211, Foxes Union of America, on the one hand, and the Hounds Association of Northern Virginia on the other. The contract expires on September 30 of each year, but it has been annually renewed with only a single strike — an eleven-day misunderstanding in 1963 — to mar an otherwise perfect record of labor relations. Local 211 is one of the oldest, most respected, and most civilized unions in this part of the country. I have never heard a bad word said of it. It is open to both red and gray foxes, without discrimination of any sort; it maintains an excellent pension and welfare fund; and except where the interests of foxes are immediately involved, the union stays resolutely aloof from political strife. It has never endorsed a candidate for public office.

The union's social occasions are highly regarded. I am indebted to Jack DeBergh, a former Master of the Rappahannock Hunt, for passing along the text of an announcement that he noticed one autumn evening while hacking home to Harris Hollow. His horse shied at a neatly mimeographed communication that came floating through the woods.

"The annual membership meeting of Local 211, FUA," this remarkable document began, "will be held in Carney's Bottom on Wednesday, September 14. Social hour at midnight. Filet of chipmunk promptly at 1 A.M. Members must advise the Secretary if they intend to bring a guest." The paper was signed by Broad Brush MacNeely, an old red fox that DeBergh knew well, having chased him for thirteen years.

DeBergh thought nothing in particular of the notice, beyond remarking that the union had changed the site of its annual meeting from Mason's Mountain to Carney's Bottom. He stuck the notice in a split branch, and hacked on home. The annual meeting, of course, is a large affair, concluding with a festive fox-trot and some rousing toasts to a good season to follow. The union's executive committee meets more frequently, but there seldom is much business to discuss.

The Hounds Association of Northern Virginia (HANOVA) is held in equal esteem. It traces its lineage to the original George Washington Hounds who hunted north and west of the Shade 200 years ago. Some earnest but misguided civil righters have complained of the HANOVA's exclusivity, in that the Association rigorously excludes 'coon hounds, deer hounds, and beagles, but the criticism is not well taken. These other hounds have well-established associations of their own, equally exclusive in their own plebeian way, and no rancor ever has been observed. Members of HANOVA meet every spring at their white-columned kennels on Thornton Hill; they have a picnic and program every Fourth of July.

These civilized amenities cannot obscure the continuing relationship between the parties. It is an adversary relationship, and can never be anything else. It is the nature of foxes to run, and of hounds to run after them, and of the Hunt to bring up the rear, looking splendid. These functions were decreed on the sixth day of Creation, and no Virginian has seen fit to tamper with them since. Thus the annual contract negotiations are serious affairs, conducted firmly but in good temper, with hard bargaining on both sides.

Members of Local 211, keeping abreast of the times, in recent years have left the really tough bargaining to an international vice president who comes down from Westchester. When the hounds' spokesman mildly objected to this novelty, the union negotiators responded that they were, after all, 20th Century foxes. The talks continued. In the current contract, which I happen to have before me on the desk, the foxes agree to be hunted on Wednesdays and Saturdays from October to April, not earlier than 10 A.M. nor later than 2 P.M., with three 10-minute rest breaks to be called at the huntsman's discretion. Each team is further entitled to four time-outs at its own request. A two-minute warning horn is to be sounded by the huntsman before the chase begins. The hounds, for their part, agree to hunt "with diligence, but without lethal intention." That is how the contract reads. In the event of snow, all engagements are cancelled, and may not be rescheduled without written notice to the Secretary.

Grievances are taken to arbitration before the tripartite Society for the Preservation of Our Foxes, but grievances have been few and sessions of SPOOF are rarely convened. Indeed, the last such meeting occurred in 1963, when two high-spirited members of the Hunt by sheer inadvertence cornered a young fox, Red Mackenzie by name, in what appeared to be a shallow groundhog hole.

We must acknowledge, even as we rue, the impetuosity of headstrong youth. The two gentlemen who figured in this lamentable incident are regarded, when sober, as being among the finest horsemen in the county. It is hard to explain their action. Perhaps the devil was in them. Instead of ignoring the hapless Mackenzie, which common courtesy would have required, they leaped from their horses with wild halloos and chased the frightened fox into a hole on Little Battle Mountain. Then they dispatched a groom to ride down to Laurel Mills for four six-packs of beer, two shovels and a mattock, and they spent a hot afternoon trying to dig the fox out. Before they were done they had a hole big enough to bury a Volkswagen in. By 5 o'clock they had run out of zeal and malt liquor alike. They threw twenty-four beer cans into the vast excavation and permitted their disgusted mounts to take them home.

The infuriated Mackenzie, needless to say, emerged cursing from the hole, smelling like Old Milwaukee, and took the matter at once to the grievance committee. The foxes' union complained bitterly that Mackenzie had suffered unspeakable trauma. The hounds' spokesman replied stiffly that his members had not participated in any way, and indeed were over near Castleton at the time. The eleven-day strike followed. Then the two chastened hunters sent a formal apology. Eventually tempers cooled, but there were hard feelings for quite some time.

Since that regrettable day, no foxes have been seriously discomfited, and only two foxes have died during hunting hours. One was struck by a truck on Route 522, a mile west of Scrabble. The other died of a heart attack on Little Mason Mountain. This remarkable record is not to be attributed wholly to altruism or to the union contract. As I mentioned earlier, our subterranean housing supply also plays a part. Our county has a population of perhaps four thousand foxes, but it has four million groundhogs, and the groundhogs have left abandoned tenements everywhere. A Rappahannock fox is seldom more than fifty yards from a sign saying "vacancy" or "to let" or "Panorama Realty." As a consequence it is no trick at all for a fox to duck into a groundhog hole, catch the 12 o'clock news, have a hot lunch, and let the field go plunging by.

Our hunts are staged with great punctilio, and with strict adherence to form and tradition; they are occasions of pride to foxes, hounds, and hunters alike. Now and then things do get a little mixed up. Few observers will ever erase the memory from their minds, however keenly they may desire to do so, of the October afternoon when the hounds were cast near Avery Faulkner's cabin a couple of miles from Woodville. There was a large field that day, splendidly turned out. Conditions were ideal.

From the north deck of our home on White Walnut Hill, we saw the field plunging at breakneck pace through the gap that separates Mason from Little Mason Mountain. Onward they came, across the Burkes' high meadow, the horses straining, the riders urging their spirited chargers over brush and rail. But something was amiss. Where, pray, were the hounds?

You will find this hard to believe, and indeed I blush to relate the dreadful tale, *but the hounds were behind the horses* — about 300 yards behind. They were crying "wait for us!" and "hold up a bit!" but the field swept on. Then, what did our incredulous eyes behold but the fox, *200 yards behind the hounds!* This happened to be the same Mackenzie who had figured in the contretemps some years before. I have never seen an angrier animal in my life. He had twisted a front paw on a stone, and was noticeably limping. Every few steps he paused to whistle through his teeth. He was shouting "you idiots!" and "come back!" and "have you lost your cotton-pickin' minds?" The embarrassing experience left Mackenzie sorely depressed. He resigned from Local 211 the following year, and the last I heard he had taken to drink.

The hound business, I tell you, is serious business. Back in the late summer of 1968, the whole Commonwealth of Virginia was torn asunder by the fight over the Old Dominion's official hound. Some of the leading combatants have died, and some have retired from the field, but the memory of that epic battle lingers gently in the archives of the mind.

To go back to the beginning, the Virginia General Assembly adopted an act in 1966 declaring the American foxhound to be the Official Dog of Virginia. We already had a State Bird, the cardinal; and a State Tree, the dogwood; and it seemed a nice idea to have a State Dog. Before lobbies could get organized for setters, pointers, 'coon dogs, or retrievers, the fox hunters had their bill out of committee and on to the floor. The vote was unanimous in the Senate and 79-10 in the House.

As a general proposition, the act creating the State Dog was well regarded here in Rappahannock. While relatively few of the gentry regularly ride to the hounds, a much larger number engage in night hunting with hounds, and everybody in Rappahannock *hears* the hounds. There is no way not to hear the hounds. Some nights it is like having a trombone octet in the bedroom. After a while you get used to it, especially if you have a buildup of wax in your ears.

Time passed, and the next step was to have some literal depiction of the Official State Dog to appear on State maps and other publications. In the summer of 1968 — it was the year of the Nixon-Humphrey campaign — two candidates appeared. One was the late great White Ella. The other was what came to be known as the Composite Hound. The State Art Commission was caught in the middle; I know this to be a fact, because my wife was a member of the Commission, and I got all this firsthand. Governor Mills Godwin was also caught in the horrid affray that developed. Before the affair was done, the political future of Virginia became involved.

The 1966 act, you will understand, did not specify any particular hound. After the law was passed, the friends of White Ella began to push her as the model for *the* hound. Their case had great merit. Whelped in 1922, White Ella was a Trigg hound, all white with lemon ears. She was owned by John D. Blair, Jr., of Richmond, a tobacco merchant. He carried her all over Virginia, Kentucky, Tennessee, and West Virginia. She won the Virginia State championship at Suffolk in 1925. Then she went on to Nashville for the Grand Nationals, ran in the snow from 7 at night until 2 in the morning, and swept the field. Two weeks later, back home in Virginia, she gave birth to seven puppies. She had what hunters call a wild goose mouth. A great hound, and no doubt about it.

Very well. Mr. Blair spent $1,500 to have White Ella's portrait painted by a Richmond artist, Mrs. June Hunter. He then went to the Governor, and Mr. Godwin, not realizing what in the world he was getting into, sort of unofficially approved the idea of White Ella's being *the* hound. It was an act of great indiscretion.

For meanwhile, another faction had developed, taking the reasonable position that the Official State Dog ought not to be any one particular hound, but rather a composite of the best features of several bench and hunting hounds. This faction, headed by C. J. Ireland, president of the Fox Hunters Association, commissioned a separate portrait, painted by C. C. Fawcett of Kirkwood, Missouri. Mr. Fawcett formerly was art director for the Ralston-Purina Company.

The question thrust before the Art Commission, and indeed before a bitterly divided Commonwealth, was, *which hound?* White Ella? Or the Composite Hound? The hound dog fight heated up at the same time the Nixon-Humphrey fight was heating up. Some of John Blair's people sent word to the Governor that if the Composite Hound appeared on State highway maps, the Democratic Party would be done for in Virginia. Mr. Ireland's troops responded with ominous whoops and hollers of their own. The Art Commission said, in effect, that it didn't give a damn which hound won the contest; the Commission's sole authority was to pass on the artistic merits, if any, of the paintings submitted to it.

Toward the end of August, while the opposing armies were getting their troops in position, Bill Lyne called up and asked did I want to go night hunting. Bill was then the Rappahannock County farm agent. He would rather hunt foxes than eat. I said sure, so we went out about 10:30 and picked up Milton Yancey, Bob Apperson, and James Alvin Compton. At a point near Alum Springs Baptist Church, over in Culpeper County just east of here, they turned out 34 hounds. It was a wet night — too wet, as it happened — and the scent didn't rise until nearly 2 A.M. Then the hounds picked up a pair of gray foxes, and the night was suddenly clamorous. A hound named Steamboat led the race, but Bill Lyne's Kelso was in there all night long.

Off and on the matter of White Ella and the Composite Hound kept coming up. I forget who was supporting whom, but we sat around for hours telling foxhound lies and listening to old Steamboat calling through the night. When I left, a little before 5 A.M., Milton Yancey was still stretched out on the hood of his old red sedan, as blissful as a deck-chair tourist on a South Pacific cruise. If your musical taste runs to brasses and woodwinds, nothing beats a night hunt in the Blue Ridge. Some of the cadenzas are scored for clarinets, and some are scored for kazoos. We have hounds who are virtuosos on the French horn, some who improvise arpeggios on the flute, and one who used to squeak like bad brake drums.

I hate to wind up the story on an anticlimactic note, but that's how it ended. The Art Commission, in a bold diplomatic stroke, accepted *both* paintings. Then Governor Godwin, I am told, quietly passed the word to the Highway Department and to the editors of various State publications: *no dog*. The next year's Official State Map appeared with only the familiar emblem of cardinal and dogwood. Nixon carried Virginia by about 150,000 over Humphrey. The traumas of the summer so affected Mills Godwin, who was then going out of office as a Democrat, that he turned himself into a Republican and four years later got himself reelected.

Mr. Blair died in May of 1976 at 83. Mr. Ireland died the following December. He was 78. The controversy itself had faded long before the old warriors passed away, but Bill Lyne swears that on soft summer nights in Piedmont Virginia, when the moon is high and the fox scent rises, you can still hear the wild goose cry of White Ella making music on the misty hills.

I don't want to leave the impression that foxhounds are

forever involved in dissension, whether with foxes or portrait painters or politicians, but one other story does come to mind. We were sitting around the kitchen fire one evening, when the matter of jury service came up and Colonel Carney recalled the first time he was called in Rappahannock County.

This was a good many years ago. It seems that a churlish old fellow, mean-tempered and generally antisocial, was living by himself way back in the hills, the other side of Meetinghouse Mountain near Ben Venue. People hated him, and he hated people, but mostly he hated hounds. The colonel couldn't recall his name. The fellow was known simply as "the hermit," or as the word is locally pronounced, "the hummit."

Now, men who follow hounds are almost always Christian gentlemen, kind and virtuous and respected, but one particular hound owner at this time was known as a devious man, sly and shifty, a little sticky fingered with other people's property. His name may have been Willy Johnson—something like that — but he wasn't even distantly related to the upstanding Johnsons around the county.

Anyhow, one night some shots were heard up at the hermit's place, just as Willy Johnson's hounds were running hard on an old gray. Sure enough, the pack had run across the old man's backyard, between the porch and the privy, and when Johnson got there his best hound was dead. Johnson had to go all the way to Warrenton to find a lawyer who would take his case, but he finally paid an attorney a full fee in advance and sued the hermit for $200 damages for shooting the dog.

The colonel was then fairly new to the county. Recognizing him as the only unbiased juror, the judge made him foreman. It was a close case in its way. The defendant pleaded property rights; after all, said the hermit, the hounds had come through his fence in full cry, hard on the heels of the fox; they had disturbed his repose and violated his right of peaceful possession. The plaintiff pleaded hound dog rights; you can't convict a hound of trespass, said Johnson; by immemorial custom hounds have rights to travel freely.

The jurors retired to consider their verdict, and the colonel

94

discovered he had a nice ethical problem on his hands. The jury was composed entirely of foxhound men. In their view, the hermit was plainly in the wrong; they were ready to award the plaintiff the full amount sued for. But — and this was the rub — it could be strongly inferred from the evidence in the case that Willy Johnson had stolen the $200 hound in the first place. Well, I asked the colonel, after a pause to kick up the kitchen fire, what did you do? The jury found for the plaintiff in the sum of $200, he said, but two weeks later a committee of five husky fellows drove over to Willy Johnson's place. Johnson came to the door, glared at them, and asked their business. They told him a volunteer fire department was being formed to protect the whole district from Flint Hill to Amissville. They had him down for a $200 contribution. The committee members looked him dead in the eye, cold as ice, and Willy Johnson got the point. He gave them the hermit's $200 check.

Rappahannock is not all foxes, foxhounds, and fox hunters, for other species are more numerous by far. This is great deer hunting country, but it is difficult deer hunting country also. This is not owing to the ruggedness of the terrain or to the incompetence of the hunters; it is rather owing to the intelligence and the foresight of the animals themselves.

I have never heard that the deer have a union of their own. They are bound together in something more like a trade association whose executive director mails an advisory in mid-October every year. The purpose of the advisory is to alert members to the opening and closing dates of the hunting season, and to suggest that they get packing. The effectiveness of this notice may be observed by the leaf-lookers who drive out from big Washington to admire our autumns, and by the frustrated home folks as well.

From mid-January to mid-October, it is no trick at all to see deer at close range. They may be found shopping in the cornfields; they dine in the apple and peach orchards; they regularly jog along the road from Ben Venue to Flint Hill. Toward the end of October, however, a remarkable exodus occurs. The deer head for the sanctuary of the National Forest in squads, platoons, companies, and whole battalions. In order to protect them from the leaf-lookers' traffic, the compassionate highway people have marked a number of "deer crossings" at especially dangerous points. The bucks ordinarily are laden with suit bags and heavy luggage; the does carry parcels of one sort or another; the yearlings bring skis and camping gear. Thanks to the advisory notice, which always is accompanied by geodetic maps, the deer know precisely where the boundaries of the National Forest begin and end. They go to campsites a quarter-mile inside the Park, and there they settle down for the two-month season. They read, sleep, engage in winter sports, enjoy Christmas; and come February or early March, about the time the sap begins to stir in the young apple trees, they troop back down the mountains.

It is all the more remarkable, therefore, that the deer harvest is as large as it is. In a normal year, 400 deer are recorded at our six game-checking stations. The figure includes about 90 does, which may seem a large number, but evidently the balance is about right. Game biologists are confident that there are far more deer in the area today than there were when Francis Thornton came our way 250 years ago.

For the record, I perhaps should add that I do no hunting myself; the only gun around our place is an antique double-barreled .410 that Ben Pietri handed down to his younger daughter; I could no more shoot a deer (or anything else, poisonous snakes excepted) than I could shoot a pet collie. But I am a hypocrite about these things. Given a crack at venison tenderloin, marinated in a good burgundy and cooked just so, I fling compunction to the wind. Most of our hunters are motivated by the prospect of meat in the freezer; they don't kill for the sake of killing.

The checking stations keep a count not only on deer but on bear also. There are more bear stories than there are bear. Deputy Sheriff Ronnie Hawkins investigated an entirely typical incident a couple of years ago. I cannot improve on the account as it appeared in the Rappahannock *News.*

> After an unusual experience last week, Deputy Hawkins finds he has far more respect for bears than he did before. Not only are they smart, they're choosy, he said. All told, during a number of trips to the freezer on the back porch at Sam and Helen Snead's in Gid Brown Hollow, the bear made off with 14 chuck roasts, a couple of pork roasts, four gallons of ice cream, several long loaves of French bread, some wild berries the Sneads had picked and some bags of store-bought vegetables, including brussel sprouts and corn.
>
> "The Sneads found some traces of paper up on the mountain after one of the earlier trips," Hawkins said. "The bacon was evidently too salty for him. They found a slab he bit off and dropped. He didn't touch the rest of the bacon in the freezer when he came back."
>
> "He just wiped 'em out of berries," Hawkins said. "They had picked the berries and wrapped them in clear paper—something like Handiwrap —to freeze. But the roasts, I don't know how he could tell what they were, they were wrapped in freezer paper. But the vegetables, they were bought at the supermarket. The bags had little pictures on them, so I guess he could identify them.
>
> "The morning Helen called me, she was real upset. When they got up they found the top to the freezer open and more food was missing. I tried to take fingerprints on the chrome handle of the freezer, but the prints had been messed up and it was excessively dirty. Inside the freezer, in the frost on the side wall, there was a lot of dirt, mud, and some scratch marks. I thought at the time it

might be a bear and those were paw prints in the frost, but I didn't say anything because Helen was so upset and she might think I was crazy or something."

So Deputy Hawkins, who lives just down the road from the Sneads, kept a stake-out on the house for a couple of hours one night. "The bear came back," he reported, "but it must have been after I'd gone, because I never saw anything. Helen called me the next morning and told me the bear woke them in the middle of the night. Sam had to go scare him off the back porch."

If you hang around the co-op or pass the time of day at the Post Office, you hear similar bear stories all the time. Up in Shenandoah National Park, bears regularly scare the wits out of campers, but in a typical hunting season only a dozen are killed. Twice I have had a go at eating bear meat, but even basted with burgundy, it isn't much.

One night we saw a wildcat on the back road to son Sean's, over near Hawlin — a yellow beast, lithe and dangerous, at once beautiful and cruel—but that was some years ago and I suspect wildcats are just about extinct. Most of our animals are less exotic and more abundant — raccoons, possums, squirrels, groundhogs, rabbits, chipmunks, and skunks.

Back in the fall of 1972, we ran into a considerable problem in diplomacy, strategy and old-fashioned hospitality. It was a problem that had to be approached with delicacy and courage, if indeed it were to be approached at all. This was the problem of Rosebud and Lord Macaulay. Skunks was their name and socializing was their game.

As I mentioned a moment ago, the general rule at our place is that the collies may kill snakes and groundhogs, because this is their nature. My wife traps mice. I swat flies, but otherwise no one kills anything. The rule is live and let live. If the human race would just observe that rule, we'd have a better human race. Here the rule works admirably for birds and animals alike, and when Rosebud and Lord Macaulay turned up, our first thought was that they too were entitled to Fifth Amendment protections, due process of law, assistance of counsel, and all the rest. But they were, as I said—well, they were skunks.

Rosebud appeared toward the end of October, along a fencerow a hundred yards from the house — a cunning creature, black as a Bible, with a whitewashed face and a white-tipped tail. She was grubbing away in the front field, minding her own business. Everybody came out on the deck to look at Rosebud, and Rosebud looked back at us. Lorenzo, who is nobody's fool, lay down and looked the other way. Rosebud waved delicately, and went back to grubbing.

Every evening for a month, along about drinking time, we could look out the back window and see Rosebud out for a stroll. When we didn't see her, we could, ah, detect her presence otherwise. Once, coming home from a good party at the Carneys, we nearly ran over her in the driveway. After that we drove up the driveway ver-r-ry slowly. If Rosebud were in the traffic pattern, we waited until the walk-and-don't-walk sign changed. Live and let live.

One evening in mid-November, we were coming home at twilight, ver-r-ry slowly up the drive, and there was her gentleman friend. Back in September, son Kevin had built an umpire's platform for the tennis tournament — a sheet of plywood nailed securely to a couple of sawhorses—and sitting on that platform, regally enthroned, haughtily surveying the turf, was the noblest skunk I have ever seen.

He had a certain air about him. You remember Macaulay? "We do not hesitate to pronounce," his lordship used to say. After a while, when it suited him and not one moment before, this skunk shinnied down from the umpire's platform and strode across the driveway. Most skunks amble, or waddle, or lumber along with the rolling gait of a sailor just in from the sea, but not this majestic being. Lord Macaulay strode.

What to do? The pair moved in. They took up housekeeping. Rosebud went shopping for linens and china. They brought in a Victorian sofa, a chest of drawers, a potted palm, and a Hong Kong chest. Lord Macaulay took to sitting around the tennis court by evening, in white ruffled shirt and black velvet jacket, smoking a thin cigar.

About this time we scheduled a flossy party for the press. Horrid premonitions raced through our heads. Imagination went to work. The mind's eye perceived the arrival of a delegation from the Washington *Post*, accompanied by *The New York Times*. Suppose they neglected to drive ver-r-ry slowly up the drive? Za-a-p! The prospect boggled the mind.

A distant authority, asked to resolve the situation, suggested by telephone that Lord Macaulay and his paramour be trapped alive and transported. Some months earlier, when the chipmunks and squirrels were stealing our bird feeders blind, I had bought two Havahart traps from Sears, Roebuck, one small, one middle-sized, but I never had the heart to set the big one and the small one caught nothing but Charlie the chipping sparrow. It caught him twice and he was plenty burned up. Besides, I wondered, how would you get a live skunk out of the trap?

We worried over the problem for a week or two, and at one point I was on the verge of asking Henry Kissinger to run out and negotiate a truce. Henry could negotiate anything. We were beginning to be afraid Lord Macaulay would hang around the tennis court forever, and would demand to referee the next Labor Day Tournament.

But everything worked out. We had underestimated the politesse of this elegant pair. On the night of the party, they stayed in their manor house until the *Post* and the *Times* had gone down the drive. Then, so help me, they appeared hand-in-hand within 20 feet of the front door. Nothing remained of the dinner but three Parker House rolls and a few scraps of salmon poached in chablis. In gratitude, I put the scraps outside in a pie pan, and the next morning the scraps were gone. Just before Christmas Rosebud and his lordship went south to Madison County for the winter. When they returned the following spring, they moved into more spacious quarters a quarter mile down the fencerow, and so far as I know, they live there quietly yet, enjoying a fine view of the mountains.

Skunks are not pests; they are at worst contingent perils, like obnoxious in-laws far away. It is possible, indeed, to say some kind things about skunks, for skunks keep the beetle population down. By contrast, rabbits, chipmunks and groundhogs are truly pests; they have no character to speak of. When God invented them, God was having an off day.

To be sure, baby rabbits are cunning creatures. They are muff brown and round-eyed; they move like two-year-old boys, bundled in snowsuits: Hop, pause; hop, pause; hop, hop, pause. The babies see the world as filled with unsensed wonder, and they are too young to be afraid. But the trouble with baby rabbits is that they grow up to be juvenile delinquents. Then they graduate from teen-aged crimes to full-blown felonies. Rabbits cannot be appeased; they are insatiable. Rabbits cannot be contained; they multiply. It is no use appealing to their better nature, for they have none.

Over the years, we have tried every technique of peaceful coexistence with the rabbit hordes. We built a Berlin Wall of chicken wire around the vegetable garden. They scorned it. They tunneled under the wall; they climbed over it rung by rung, like Marines up a rope ladder; they hurled themselves against the wall until they breached the barricade. *And they laughed!* Have you ever been snickered at by fifteen knee-slapping rabbits? Few sneers are more contemptuous.

We bought great strips of mesh from the Burpee people, and draped the early spring peas in nylon net. The nets were supposed to be rabbit-proof. Nonsense. Two buck rabbits appeared, as big as bull calves. They had teeth like the teeth on a front-end loader. In three nights they chewed the nets to rags and tatters. Then they ate the peas and swaggered away, thumbs in their jeans, *and laughing.*

We tried the friendly approach. Brotherhood. The whole bit. We dismantled most of the useless Berlin Wall and took to leaving the garden gate ajar. We posted hospitable signs: Rabbits Welcome Here. *Ici on parle lapin.* Two rows of lettuce were labeled "Salad Bar." The general idea was that if we took the fun out of felony—if we decriminalized the business of raiding our garden—the rabbits would grow bored; there would be no challenge, no sport, nothing but wholesome meals, planned recreation, and balanced nutrition. It was a bootless idea. The rabbits stopped laughing — that much was gain — but natural-born freeloaders can never be reformed. Neither can their manners be improved. Ten months out of the year, whether the garden is ripe or barren, the rabbits still stroll around to taunt the collies; they stick out their tongues, they waggle fingers in their ears, they yell, "yanh, yanh, you can't catch me." Every summer we hope we have seen our last one hundred thousand rabbits, but every summer sees the tribe increase. Somehow the garden survives.

Rabbits can be eaten, of course, and when they are raised on a diet of hybrid broccoli, blue lake bush beans, Waltham asparagus, and oak leaf lettuce, they are as tender as corn-fed chickens. Commercially, their fur may have some value. There was a time when their feet were marketed as good luck charms. That is the best that can be said for rabbits. Chipmunks and groundhogs fail even in these departments. The chipmunks fly across the lawn, tails high, like little sailboats on a gusty lake. They have an unerring instinct for the most expensive iris and the rarest lily bulbs. They play steeplechase games on the stone fences. It does no good to drop camphor balls down chipmunk holes; the chipmunks think you want to play ping-pong.

Groundhogs are to chipmunks as bulldozers are to garden tractors. Groundhogs are burly fellows, broad-shouldered, paunchy, generally illiterate, indifferent to the finer amenities of life. They dig prodigious holes, a foot or so in diameter at the surface, and they dig not one hole but three or four. It is all they have to do. Otherwise they would be wholly unemployed. After digging for three or four hours in the early morning, they sit on the front porch in their undershirts and baggy pants. At noon they waddle down the fencerow for a couple of beers. Then they nap, or go bowling. In the evenings they watch reruns of "All in the Family." Archie Bunker is their guy. Their taste in literature seldom rises above Moon Mullins. Musically speaking, they are indifferent—blue grass, country western, hillbilly, it is all the same, anything with a little tune to it. Very few groundhogs have benefited from higher education; almost all of them played two years of high school football, generally as defensive linemen, and then dropped out. Like many a fat man on a tennis court, the groundhog is deceptively fast. Perhaps the early athletic training has something to do with it.

The groundhog also is known as the woodchuck, which may explain why so many of the males are named Charlie. The females generally have two names — Annie Mae, Lou Belle, Rhoda Sue, and the like, but not infrequently one is introduced to a Lurline, Darlene, or Laurine. Like the males, the females tend to put on too much weight; they go quickly to flab and lack the character to diet. They are known, however, as devoted mothers; they have good taste in fresh vegetables, especially Burpee's hybrid zucchini; most of them go to church on Sundays. I have tried to be just in these observations, but that is about all that can be said for the groundhog.

No examination of our fauna would be complete without a word or two on our domesticated beasts. These are almost entirely beef cattle. Rurally speaking, ours is a cow-calf economy. In the whole of Rappahannock County, not more than 15 or 20 farmers raise feeder pigs. About the same number, maybe fewer, raise sheep, but Lois Snead, the judge's wife, is the only one with a significant operation. This is a pity, too, for our steep limestone hills are ideally suited for raising sheep, and it makes little sense to have to drive in to the Culpeper Safeway to buy lamb from New Zealand. It's the same story with dairy farming. There used to be two good-sized dairy operations, but as I write in 1977 there is none. Only a few households still keep milk cows for home consumption — granddaughter Heather was introduced to their enduring fascination the summer she was four. Quite a few horse breeders still pursue their risky enterprise.

Otherwise it's cattle. In 1966, when we first came to Rappahannock, it was all Black Angus. You never saw anything else. Then Allen Stokes developed a purebred Charolais operation, and the Manwarings began experimenting with Charolais crosses. Some Herefords came in. A number of breeders got into Angus-Hereford crosses, and we began seeing calves that looked as if they had come from a minstrel show — black bodies and chalk-white faces. All told, we have maybe 13,000 head of cattle and calves in an average year; this is nothing by Texas standards, but for its size Rappahannock ranks all right among our beef-producing counties.

When everything goes well, there's both pleasure and profit in raising cattle. The trouble is that everything seldom does go well. In the summer of 1976, for example, we went weeks without rain; the meadows dried up and the hay crops were pitiful. Then came the bitter winter, with the pastures locked in snow and ice. Taking care of the animals was a brutal business. At the same time the markets were touching bottom. A number of calves froze to death. Under such conditions, raising cattle isn't a profitable enterprise; it's more of an expensive, exhausting hobby, and you wonder why the beef producers stick with it. You don't have to be crazy to be a farmer, as they say, but it helps you overlook the pain.

I do not get along with cows, to confess the uncomfortable truth, and this is so whether we are talking of Charlies, Herefords, or Black Angus. There is simply no communication. It may have something to do with poor eyesight, I don't know, but my impression is that steers read very little; they probably read less than groundhogs read, and they almost never watch TV. Only a few of the activist calves ever bother to vote; probably 95 per cent of the herds do not follow politics at all. As a consequence, we have nothing in common. Nothing whatever. The cows see me as an ignorant dilettante from the big city; I see them as a bunch of dumb country bumpkins. The animus is mutual.

But some people have a way with cows. I learned this on a

Sunday morning in November, a few years ago. Marie was in Italy with her sister, having an all-girl holiday, and Lorenzo and I were baching it, if that's how you spell the verb. I had dressed for church, and we were sitting contentedly around the kitchen fire, waiting for 10:30. Lorenzo was showing me his perfect profile. He is the handsomest collie in the world, and he knows it. He will tell you so. Ask him sometime.

All of a sudden this vainglorious Barrymore leaped to his feet, in a torrent of furious barking, and behold: Just outside the big windows, right on the lawn, munching their way toward the wild flower garden, were three Black Angus cows and two black calves. Lorenzo was hollering "Trespassers!" and "Call John Walker Jenkins!" He was leaping at the door, trying to get at them. I opened the door and he flew outside, with me just behind. I was waving a crooked cane and yelling. We were brave as lions. Whereupon the lead cow charged, spilling the bird feeder as it came.

Well, Barrymore fled behind the woodpile. I retreated to the kitchen and telephoned Garfield Burke, which is what one always did in such an emergency, and went to change out of my church clothes. When I returned to the arena, Lorenzo had come off the bench. He had driven the opposing team fifty yards downfield. There they stood under a dogwood, huddling and glowering, heads down, shuffling their feet, waiting for play to resume. We were eyeball to eyeball.

Then Garfield arrived in his pickup truck, put on his boots, and went over to the enemy huddle. He said to those cows, very softly, "Hoo, there." That was all. "Hoo, there." The lead cow must have weighed a thousand pounds. Maybe twice that much. The other two were almost as big. Counting the calves, maybe five or ten tons of beef on the hoof were ready to charge. Once more he said, "Hoo, there." They turned on their heels, these behemoths, and trotted docilely up the fencerow, back to their locker room, with Lorenzo, triumphant, fifty yards behind. Then I helped Garfield patch up the fence, and we talked a little politics, and he went on home. Some time later, when I had a stout three-rail fence between me and

105

them, I tried saying "Hoo, there," to a couple of cows, but they paid no attention. Black Angus cattle do not talk to me.

A part of the enduring fascination of country living lies in the cycles, or rhythms, of rural existence. We see these in the crops, the wild flowers, the vegetable garden, the soft uncurling of the leaves, like baby toes, in early spring. We see it, of course, in the animals also.

Just before Christmas of 1972, at a few minutes past 8 o'clock of a Monday morning, a black calf was born in Mr. Burke's field just across the ravine. Later that same morning, we saw a redpoll at Charlie's Bar & Grill. The following day some astronauts came home from the moon. A few days later, on Saturday, Christmas Eve, we marked the shortest day of the year. Somehow the disparate events all fit together.

Considering that we have more than twice as many cows and calves as we have people, the birth of a Black Angus calf is nothing to call the Rappahannock *News* about. Neither was there anything exceptional about that Monday morning. It was bitterly cold. When I went outside at 7:15, to bring in some firewood and to hoist a flag on the Number Two pole, a north wind snatched at the banner, and the flag flapped like a great wild bird in my hands.

On the ridge cross the ravine, in black silhouette against the sullen sky, the cow lay in labor. She was stretched on her right side, belly heaving, her dark head pushing and straining against the ground. I put the kindling on the hearth. Marie was at the glass door, watching the cow a hundred yards away. "I think we're having a calf," she said.

Up in New York City, a thousand light years to the east, Frank McGee and Barbara Walters were chatting about the morning news: The astronauts were heading home, with bags of moon rocks in their ships; U. S. bombers had resumed their raids on North Vietnam; a father of four had been slain on a Belfast street. The cow got heavily to her feet, stumbled a step or two, lay down again.

At 8:13 or thereabouts, the calf was born. It was a small calf, black as the lunar space beyond the moon. On the frozen hill the afterbirth produced a milky steam. The calf lay for a minute or so, being licked; then it tried its front legs, and discovered they worked; and tried its back legs, and discovered they worked too. The calf discovered milk, and began to nurse. How did these instincts get programmed into a newborn calf? Who put the instincts there? Half an hour later, when I happened to glance again that way, the cow and calf had ambled off.

A little before noon, when I went to the kitchen to fetch a forgotten book, Marie was looking intently through the glass door again. She was watching the bird feeder that hangs from the chestnut oak. "New customer," she said. Sure enough, there at Charlie's Bar & Grill, ordinarily patronized by sparrows, juncos, cardinals, bluejays and evening grosbeaks, was a small stranger — red-capped, rose-breasted, yellow-beaked, black-masked. Marie reached for the bird book on her desk.

"The Common Redpoll breeds in the Northern Hemisphere from the tundra south; in North America to s. Newfoundland, n. c. Quebec, n. Manitoba, and n. British Columbia ... In winter irregularly south to North Carolina, n. Oklahoma, Colorado, and n. California."

It had flown a long way, this most uncommon redpoll, and would fly a long way back again, with God knows what computer in its tiny head. On Tuesday afternoon the astronauts came home, bringing the red-orange evidence they had sought: Some eons back, out of the depths of the silent lunar mass, a fumarole had vented, freezing a tear in the eye of the moon. On Saturday the sun rose at 7:20 and set at 4:39.

I fell to thinking about all this as I worked on the mail. There was a letter from a friend in Kansas, a teacher gone recently into business. He was concerned at the demands of his new work. "I hope that I won't wake up one day," he wrote, "and find I've missed the point."

It does no harm to think upon these things. What is the point? The point is to understand, if we can, the wild, sublime design of man and the world he inhabits. By "wild," I mean to suggest the unchecked, unsaddled course of *homo sapiens,* the good and evil all combined: worlds explored and peasants slain, live orphans and dead moons, barbarians and astronauts. Man is wild, and man is sublime, and so is the grand design. How came the fumarole? How came the astronauts? Any farmer can tell you how a calf is born; and yet he cannot truly tell you how a calf is born. Husbandry and mystery are not the same. In the space of a few days, we marked the birth of a small black calf, the flight of a bird no bigger than a finch, the spoor of eons, the turning of a planet on an axis. And just before Christmas, right on schedule, one minute at a time, the days grew longer.

I wrote to my friend in Kansas, stumbling over words as I have stumbled here, and spoke of a newsman's necessary bondage to Washington and New York. "There," I said, "is where the action is. But here in the hills—ah, here in the hills is the point."

Ordinarily the birds evoke no such metaphysical reflections. The birds are pure delight.

The spring after we moved into the new house, we hung a bird feeder just outside the kitchen. It swiftly became the neighborhood pub, owned and operated by Charlie the chipping sparrow. He was a tough little redheaded character. He wanted his patrons to enjoy themselves, but he ran an orderly house. Early and late Charlie tended his bar, polishing the brasses, tidying up the spilled seed, listening to the titmice chatter. He kept strict hours, got along well with the bluejay cops, and never gave us a day of trouble. Charlie was the first of the birds we came to know on a first-name basis. Another was Billy the Kid. The young Arnold couple, Matthew and Frances, stayed with us for several years.

I got the theme for a whole essay out of Billy the Kid. He was a big blue grosbeak who arrived right after May Day every year. He was punch-drunk, and got punchier with every passing season. We would be wakened in the morning by an imperious pounding on the windowpane. There on the sill, this old club fighter would be battering at his image in the glass. He used to spend hours, staggering from one window to another. At every point he confronted another blue grosbeak precisely as big as himself. He fought all morning long, hurling himself headfirst upon his antagonist, backing away, and slugging some more. Two hundred fights a morning left him giddy but unbowed. His head must have rung like a Chinese gong. Afternoons he used to hang around Charlie's Bar & Grill, bragging to the cowbirds that he could lick any guy in the house. So much truculence! So much frustration! Billy retired from the ring in 1974, but a year or so later his son returned in his place. Bill, Jr., had a good right jab, but he never showed the form of his dad.

In February of 1976 we put a classified ad in *Saturday Review,* on the reasonable surmise that most bluebirds read Norman Cousins, and a few days later a handsome young male turned up. This was Matthew Arnold, who had flown in to inspect the premises with a view toward renting a house for the summer. Ordinarily we don't start showing the bluebird houses until St. Patrick's Day or thereabouts, but this was an exceptional winter in the mountains. Usually we have to apologize for February, a dull, dour month with nothing to do and four bleak weeks to do it in. But in 1976, so they said, the Postal Service got February mixed up with March, and they sent us some days in the 70's a month before they were due.

Young Arnold arrived a little before 8 o'clock, while Marie was having her second cup of coffee. He knocked diffidently at the big glass door, and at first I thought it was a chickadee looking for a piece of toast and jelly. Then I saw the burgundy turtleneck and the spiffy sports coat, and Marie went to get the keys. Our bluebird houses were made by the Boy Scouts of Amissville of rough-cut pine, with wall-to-wall carpet and Waverly fabric in the draperies. We advertise them with refrig., air cond., washer & drier, magnif view of mtns, all utils frnshd, and they rent fast.

Arnold had the newlywed flutters that morning. He was trying to be dignified, and picky and choosy, and he wondered if Frances would be happy with the electric stove, but he kept saying "gosh!" and "it *is* a lovely view." Two weeks later his bride flew in, very chic and slender, and the following year she started a bridge club and Arnold became president of the PTA.

Ours is a great county for retired military people, which may account for the number of military birds who come our way. Our robins move as precisely as a good Marine Corps band. We have sergeant major blackbirds, crimson chevrons on their sleeves. The flickers come sashed and medaled, in the fashion of Bolivian generals. Our downy woodpeckers are striped-shirt sailors, eating their fill at a suet bar.

If I have a favorite bird, it's probably the titmouse. Titmice have class. But the indigo bunting is a beauty. The chickadees are as much fun as grandchildren. There's a lot to be said for the finches. If you haven't watched a nuthatch come headfirst down the trunk of a tree, you've missed a splendid circus performance. The killdeers (they are known in our hills as kildees) are great actors but silly home builders; their idea of a fine homesite is in the gravel shoulder of a driveway. The golden-crowned kinglet often shows up for the Christmas holidays, wearing its party clothes. A few weeks later we get invaded by evening grosbeaks in yellow slacks, panama boaters and linen sports coats, on their way to Florida for the season. We have warblers, wrens, hummingbirds, thrashers, meadowlarks, orioles in rose chiffon. And of course we have the quail, wearing their Helen Hokinson hats. I don't know how it is elsewhere, but all our hen quail belong to the D.A.R., and the cock quail are pillars of the Union Club.

Every society has its criminal elements. Ours come by the name of cowbirds. Maybe they have a useful place in the ornithological scheme of things, but it's hard to think what that place may be. Cowbirds are somber creatures, hooded like executioners; there is nothing larky about them. They are deeply into gambling, hard narcotics, nest-snatching, and the loan shark racket. One summer a couple of cowbirds muscled in on Bluebird Row, evicted the lawful tenants, and dared anyone to move them out. A few weeks later they hatched some young; we could hear the fledglings peeping inside. The next day a five-foot black snake came gliding through the grass, swiveled up the fence pole, stuck his head inside, and opened his jaws. In a few minutes the snake backed out and slithered away. We watched the horrid infanticide from the deck, without lifting a finger to interfere with the snake. Maybe I should have run for a sharp-edged hoe, but the incident had elements of justice.

After I wrote about this in a column, dozens of readers wrote in to say that cowbirds don't raise their own young; they lay their eggs in others' nests and let somebody else do the job. This doubtless is true as a general rule, but there are seven species of cowbirds, and these Rappahannock racketeers may be different. Anyhow, that's what happened. I felt a little guilty, but after cocktail time that afternoon the feeling had gone away. Unfortunately, the cowbirds stayed around all summer.

With the coming of autumn, we see changes in the bird and animal life. Some of our tenants, including the despised cowbirds, drift away. Swallows and kildees and phoebes pack up their valuables, close their houses, and depart. Day by day, tree by tree, the mountains take on their fall coloration.

They say that our autumns are like wine, here in the Blue Ridge, and the simile contains both truth and poetry. Wines come in vintage years, some poor, some good, some great. A truly great autumn, such as the autumn of 1972, is money in the bank. When the word goes out that our maples are brilliant crimson and the gums a burgundy red; when the oaks and hickories and persimmons turn early; when the poplars and white walnuts carpet the country lanes in gold—then the heart lifts up, and so does local trade. "Come sip our autumn," we say. "This is a great one."

I mark the '72 vintage especially. I had been out on the campaign trail for a part of October, covering McGovern and

Nixon, and trudged home a weary correspondent. The hills were a tonic to the drooping spirit. We had had heavy rains in September, and these washed the roadside foliage free of dust. On October 21 came a sudden frost, spread over the fields like a clean white sheet. All the campaign rhetoric disappeared. We termed it the burgundy fall.

Rudasill's Mill Road, leading down to Woodville, was petaled in brown and green and gold. One walked through a long cathedral aisle, vaulted in dark beams, great shafts of sunlight striking through the heavy oaks. At the bend, just across White Walnut Run, a towering maple made a scarlet sanctuary. Down Red Oak Mountain came a procession, as in solemn high mass, acolytes in black cassocks, priests in richly figured chasubles, mitered bishops, a sumac cardinal.

Such an autumn is an exercise for the painter, not the writer. One counts the colors: Green, of course, but a green that is wholly different from the tints of spring — a somber green, verging close to black. Against the greens the palette holds half a dozen browns — dark brown, dull brown, cordovan, the brown of stained old slippers, a birch that surrenders leaves of creamy beige. The browns yield to rusty reds — to crimson, russet, burnt umber. The reds sparkle with yellows, the yellow of lemons, the softer gleam of copper pots well rubbed. Stalks of uncut corn, like gaunt old soldiers clad in faded khaki, stand in ragged array.

When it rains in a vintage fall, the image is not of cathedrals, but of Camelots. Wet leaves in the sunshine turn to burnished armor. In the first light of morning, the poorest stalk is a gleaming lance of ice; the mountains turn to tapestries, the last red and golden leaves to pennons hanging over banquet halls. We have known these bronze Octobers. They glisten and they gleam; one looks for chain mail knights to joust for passage at a country bridge.

This is the way it is, perhaps one autumn out of three — October marching like a Big Ten band, the willows strutting like majorettes, the elms and maples with a trumpet glory all their own. Other autumns, to confess the truth, are something less. They are old books, the dark morocco stamped with fading gold; they are dusty boots, pressed roses, freckled hands that flutter feebly. We ought never to boast too much.

Even so, there is no such thing as a bad autumn in the Blue Ridge. It becomes possible to walk softly in the shadowed woods, an inquisitive collie now in front and now behind. You pause to pick up an acorn from the forest floor. The acorn cracks; and buried within the ivory flesh one sees the infant beams, the ribs of unbuilt ships. Walnuts emerge damp-black from spongy wombs. These are not days of death in the woods; these are days of conception, the seed dropping, the wet mold covering, the earth enfolding in winter's slow gestation.

One October two young ladies came to stay in the cottage over a weekend. They went out with Lorenzo and Piper, down to the neglected apple orchard, to see if a few Yorks remained on the tree by the fencerow. They returned, quite forgetting the apples, with a basket of things: A sprig of sumac, pinot noir; goldenrod, chablis; white asters, pale as dry champagne. They had gathered a tiny sassafras, its cane-headed root smelling of all the root beer ever compounded. They had leaves, grass, corn stubble, thistles; they had dogwood berries, black-tipped, red as traffic lights; they had pokeberries, persimmons, holly, running cedar, a mottled feather from a pheasant's breast.

They tumbled their basket on an old pine table, and abruptly all of autumn occupied the room. It was time to pry open the walnut with a kitchen knife, to test the persimmon gently on the tongue. There was a grasshopper still clutching the sassafras limb, jeweled as a green enamel in Tiffany's window. They had brought home a passenger caterpillar too, black and russet, fur soft. We looked at these miracles by lamplight in the late afternoon, seeing the promise of summer in a dogwood bud, and after a while we gathered up the fragments and laid them, with a certain ceremony, on the compost pile.

After Christmas comes the waiting time. The chipmunks and groundhogs take to their holes. The nights drop far below freezing and the pale days seldom get above. Every morning the ice has to be broken out of the dogs' water bucket. Every night the kitchen fire must be banked.

It is pointless to hurry in the waiting time. There is no place to go. Beyond splitting and fetching firewood, few outside chores cry out to be done. After dinner, with the dishes washed, one thinks of Rupert Brooke: "These I have loved: White plates and cups, clean-gleaming." One does the small domestic things that mark the ritual hours; and one watches the sparrows and juncos and quail; and waits.

These are the sepia days, as if the engravers had done their work for rotogravure. In the far distance the mountains slumber like old men, white-haired. Closer in, the listless sun has melted patches of snow from the high meadow, and the fields are a Hereford's hide, part brown, part white. Burke's pond is a gray slick stone set in dull gold. Nothing moves, nothing but the thin smoke that rises and faintly ripples from a chimney, nothing but the school bus twice a day, nothing but the hungry, insatiable birds.

Meanwhile, the seed catalogs. They are an indispensable part of the waiting time. We could never survive the Januaries without them. Out of the gleaming ice, the mind's eye sees a crocus peeping. We make lists of lettuce, cantaloupes, tomatoes, butter beans; lists of eggplant, cucumbers, carrots, early peas, a midget corn; lists of zinnias large as pie plates, of delphiniums, marigolds, geraniums, dianthuses. "All are beautiful, hardy, and live and bloom freely." They are flowering specimens of the ad-writer's art.

There are books to be read in the waiting time, and birds to watch, and letters to write, and puzzles to put together, and loving humans to be loved. At sunset, one takes in the flags. They come to my arms in a burst of color, the flag of Virginia, the flag of my country, clean-cold, still breathing of the crisp air they have flown in. I fold them, and put them away, and return to the kitchen fire and the waiting time. I once wrote after such a day that I had not earned a penny since morning, but I was richer than I had been the night before.

Part Four

Which deals, as promised,
mostly with things botanical.

Back in 1946, as a young reporter covering the Virginia General Assembly, I tried to work up a constructive venture with a pixie legislator by the name of Lake Triplett. My thought was to have him sponsor a bill to abolish February.

The project never got off the ground. It was not that Lake thought poorly of the idea. He thought the idea altogether splendid. It was precisely his kind of idea. He was a big, tall, fatherly kind of fellow, with a face like a loaf of unbaked bread. One of his purposes in legislative life was to leaven the proceedings with a touch of levity.

At the time I approached him, he was deeply involved with his famous no-work bill. This was a bill to make it a felony in Virginia for any person to engage in a useful occupation. The bill had been sent by the Speaker to the Committee on Retrenchment and Economy, which was something of a joke in itself. This was the committee to which all the Republican members were assigned. The committee had not met for 30 or 40 years, chiefly because no bills had ever been sent to it for consideration. In order to take up Lake's bill, and to give it the careful study it plainly deserved, the committee had to borrow a vacant room and an idle clerk. The hearings, Lake told me, doubtless would consume several days and would fully occupy his attention for the remainder of the session. He was sorry. As it turned out, the committee unanimously reported his bill to the floor, where it was vigorously defended and opposed; then the House voted 99-1 to recommit the bill to the Committee on Mining and Manufactures where, alas, it died. Two years later Lake introduced a bill to regulate the depth to which snow could fall in Fairfax County. But I digress.

The bill I had drafted for Lake's approval still impresses me as a commendable exercise in the legislative art. It began by forthrightly abolishing February altogether. A second section directed that 14 days be added to April, six days to May, and five to October, with the other three or four to be assigned by the Speaker of the House and the President of the Senate. A final section relocated the birthdays of George Washington and William Henry Harrison for appropriate observance in

March and August respectively. The bill made no provision for rescheduling the birthday of Mr. Lincoln; this was in 1946, the War had been over for barely 80 years, and the strong emotions of Appomattox had not as yet subsided. It seemed to me that no member of the General Assembly could oppose so humane a measure.

Does February have a redeeming feature? The question answers itself. Perhaps once in 15 or 20 years, owing to the weathermen's inadvertence, February produces a few balmy days. Otherwise the skies sniffle, sulk, and weep. It snows, it rains, it sleets, it drizzle-drazzles. The house smells of wet collies. Firewood refuses to ignite. Certainly such a month should be abolished.

We are sustained, as I was remarking a few pages back, chiefly by the seed catalogs—by the glad tidings that come in the post from David, Joseph, Henry, and George. They are among the apostles of spring: David Burpee, Joseph Harris, Henry Field, and George Park. To say that these merchants sell seeds is to put the matter crassly. They sell dreams; they market the promise of summer.

It is a familiar theme of the off season, I know, for country folk to rhapsodize about the seed catalogs. This is a ritual text for editors with large rural circulations; come February, every such editor writes the seed catalog piece. But the missionary role of these apostolic fathers is so important to the house-bound housewife in the hills that I willingly risk a charge of banality to express a debt of gratitude here. Pray, Father Burpee, how did the pioneers make it without you?

We sit in the kitchen, after the dishes are done, with pencils and memo pads and last year's garden register, and we pore over the catalogs in a happy agony of indecision. The register reminds us that last year's cauliflower was a failure. The plants would not head up, and when a couple of them did head up, they had to be wrapped in bandanas, like aching jaws, to ward off the sun. Piper, the number two collie, kept swiping the bandanas to play tug-of-war with Lorenzo. The register tells us: Heads of cauliflower, none. But, ah! The

119

apostle Joseph, which is to say, Mr. Harris of Rochester, is offering a new, self-blanching variety: "When grown in cool weather, the wrapper leaves curl over the heads, protecting them from sunlight. Finest quality and type, deep, smooth, and pure white." Once more tempted, we write the cauliflower down: Pkt., 45 cents.

So it goes through bean (pole and bush), lettuce, melons, peppers, squashes, zucchini. In the glowing embers of the winter fire we see the cantaloupes of summer. This is decision-making of a high order, and it is not confined to half-frozen farmers on isolated country roads. The venerable American Seed Trade Association, one of the nation's oldest trade groups, regularly reports heavy orders from city gardeners as well. It may be the high price of food that has produced this urban interest, but I have a notion that a deeper motivation also plays a part. The typical city dweller lives most of his life at the mercy of other men, in bondage to faceless machines — bus drivers, repairmen, government inspectors; lathes, computers, typewriters, drill presses, bulldozers. The backyard gardener who successfully produces a row of Henry Field's buttercrunch bibb lettuce (crisp leaves are thick and juicy) may have saved a couple of dollars off his food bill, but that is the least of his achievements. This is *his* lettuce, his very own small miracle, watered and nursed and tended and finally brought to harvest. The Iowa farmer, gazing with satisfaction on 500 acres of corn, is not more proud.

Some of these subconscious stirrings may account for the reported shift in population trends. In the 1970's, the tidal movement of our people from farm to city apparently began to ebb. A perceptible trickle can be seen from the big cities back to small towns. Families are following some curious invisible string that ties them to the land, and to a sense of place. I am wary of pat explanations and glib essays on "our changing life-styles," and I doubt that the trend should be read as any very significant rejection of material comforts, but something is going on. It may be a matter of scale and relationship, a turning away from the large and the impersonal to the small and the intimate. If so, the prophets of doom are wrong: We are not moving toward an Orwellian *1984*, but back to Mr. Longfellow's spreading chestnut tree instead.

The only thing to be said for February, to get back on course, is that it ends. In Rappahannock County, the waiting time ends with it. The robins march in. Charlie the chipping sparrow returns to his bar and grill. The groundhogs emerge, carpet beaters in hand, to shake off the mud of winter. The crocus come out, innocent as cherubim, and the daffodils edge slowly onto stage. In the rock garden, tiny things peep forth — anemones, grape hyacinths, trout lilies, plants with clustered petals pink as Caribbean coral.

It is a well known fact, attested by Virginians of all ages, that Virginia has the most beautiful springs in the American Republic. Only South Carolina compares, and it does not compare often. Our springs are not always the same; that is one of their infinite delights. In some years, April bursts upon our hills in one prodigious leap — and all the stage is filled at once, whole choruses of tulips, arabesques of forsythia, cadenzas of flowering plum. The trees grow leaves overnight.

In other years, spring tiptoes in. It pauses, overcome by shyness, like a grandchild at the door, peeping in, ducking out of sight, giggling in the hallway. "Heather!" I want to cry, "I know you're out there. Come in!" And April slips into our arms. The dogwood bud, pale green, is inlaid with russet markings. Within the perfect cup, a score of clustered seeds are nestled. One examines the bud in awe: Where were those seeds a month ago? The maples do not come forth in green; they are flowering red, soft as slippers, in tassels like a jester's scepter. The flowering almond is pink, absurdly pink, little girl pink, as pink as peppermint and cream. The apples display their milliner's scraps of ivory silk, rose-tinged. All the sleeping things wake up — primrose, baby iris, candytuft, blue phlox, the Scotch heather that had seemed dead beyond resurrection. The earth warms — you can smell it, feel it, crumble

April in your hands. Our dark mountains, great-hipped, big-breasted, slumber on the western sky, their massive bulk as still as bronze by Henry Moore; and then they stretch and gradually awaken. A warm wind, soft as a girl's hair, moves sailboat clouds in gentle skies. The rains come—good rains to sleep by — and fields that were dun as oatmeal turn to pale green, then to Kelly green. More daffodils! They form a marching band of golden sousaphones. Wild strawberries! They nestle on the hillside, rubies tumbled from a jeweler's tray. Fresh mint! Parsley, thyme, chives!

Is it perfect? Not quite. Every spring my friend Geoghegan sits on the sitting bench outside the office, pondering a way to make a fortune from dandelions and wild onions. One of these days he will figure this out; when he does, we will harvest a million dollar crop in a single afternoon and sit on the porch all summer. We still have to fight the rabbit legions; the chipmunks get to be a nuisance; sometimes the spring rains produce little but spring mud; we suffer killing frosts that cause terrible damage. These detract from the sublimity of spring in Virginia, but they seldom detract severely. The just short of perfect, said Mr. George Gissing, how perfect it is!

A part of the joy of country living — a joy that can be experienced but feebly in the city—lies in the endless variety of growing things. I mean that: "endless." The botanist has not been born who can complete a glossary of God's incredible inventiveness along a country road. In spring the roadsides are painted in pastels—in chartreuse, and rose, and dogwood ivory. By early summer they take on school color hues of vivid orange and blue, day lilies and lupine. After the first cutting of hay, the pastures spring up daisy-dappled, house paint white. Beneath a parasol of Queen Anne's lace a caterpillar curls and stretches. The chicory comes and goes, flag blue, to be followed by summer asters. Actually they are not asters; they are fleabane — tiny white flowers, dime-sized, eyelash fringed, with old gold centers. The botanical name is *Erigeron*, out of the Greek for "early old man." That is to say, they are prematurely white. There is no controlling the honeysuckle; there is

no curbing the trumpet vine. To compensate for their sprawling profusion, we get tiny things in large abundance —
mayapples, buttercups, bird's-foot violets, a thousand ferns
as delicately fashioned as the eyelashes of a child. The trillium, loveliest of them all, kneels as modestly as a spring
bride, all in white, beside the altar of an old oak stump. If
you're not familiar with the trillium, imagine the flower that
would come from a flute if a flute could make a flower. That is
the trillium, a work of God from a theme by Mozart.

It is a labor of love — it is more truly an act of love — to
identify the wild flowers and to marvel at the purity of their
grace and color. Their common names bespeak a common
affection. How could Bouncing Bet be called anything else? Or
Dutchman's-Britches? Or Johnny-Jump-Up? Or Confederate
Violets? Or Basket-of-Gold? Marie has made herself an authority on the roadside flowers. As I drive along the back
roads, she keeps up a running commentary: Purslane,
storksbill, fireweed, Indian pipe! Hey, pipsissewa! You ought
to smell it! Forget-me-not, touch-me-not, sneezeweed, gen-
tian. Once she nearly wrecked us. We were driving across
northern Florida, somewhere between Tallahassee and
Gainesville, when my absentminded meditations were abruptly broken. "Hey!" she cried. "There's a naked lady!" It was
the adamasco lily — at least I think it was.

These are the highest works of the jeweler's art, these
flowers by the road. In hothouse or city garden, camellias are
marvelously satisfying flowers. A spray of dendrobium orchids can melt your heart. The hybrid azaleas and rhododendrons are lovely. We have grown iris of a positively erotic
sensuality. I don't mean to minimize the beauty of lilies, roses,
geraniums, poppies, or anything else. All I'm saying is that the
most delicate beauty, and the most perfect grace, often are
found in the humblest plants along the way. There's a moral in
all this, I suppose, but I pass it by.

Plants get to you. Four or five Christmases ago, my sister
Patsy sent us a book. It didn't exactly change our lives, but it
certainly made them chattier. The book was *The Secret Life of*

Plants by Peter Tompkins and Christopher Bird. By the time we had finished this work, Marie was talking to the philodendrons and I was arguing politics with Livingston. Livingston is the rubber tree. He has a brass nameplate on the half-barrel he lives in.

Maybe you've read the Tompkins-Bird book. The authors begin their account with the experiments of Cleve Backster, a lie detector examiner. It appears that back in 1966, out of sheer curiosity, Backster hooked up his polygraph to a dracaena in his office. The dracaena is a kind of potted palm, sometimes called the dragon tree. To Backster's amazement, when he watered the plant, the polygraph registered emotion. The plant was saying, "thank you." When Backster thought about burning a leaf with a match, the polygraph registered panic. The plant was saying, "you beast!"

Other experiments followed, in the United States, in the Soviet Union, in India and elsewhere. What the experiments appeared to indicate is that plants have feelings. Plants are afraid of pain; they respond to affection; they have varied tastes in music; they suffer from the sulks, the blues, and the blahs. When they drink too much, they complain of wet feet.

Marie read the book first. I was down at the greenhouse one morning, puttering around with an avocado that was looking a little jaundiced, and I didn't pay much attention when she came in.

"Good morning, Phil," she cried. I looked around. My name isn't Phil. She was talking to a philodendron. "Howza boy?" she asked. "Sleep well?" The next thing I knew, she was patting the leaves of a Finlandia camellia. "Just look at your new growth," she gushed. She went to an aloe. "How are all the babies this morning?" I thought she had gone bananas.

"Don't think that," she said firmly. "The bird-of-paradise knows exactly what you're thinking. It doesn't like it." Sure enough, the bird-of-paradise was plainly offended. A hanging geranium was curling its lip. The lemon tree looked sour.

After that, I read the book. Since then we've had the gabbiest greenhouse in the whole of Rappahannock County. We had been talking to the birds and to the collies all along, but the birds are flighty and the collies aren't interested in much besides college football and local politics. Once you get to know them, plants will talk about anything. Livingston, for example, is an old Republican type, the Barry Goldwater of the greenhouse. On the day after Jimmy Carter pardoned the draft dodgers, Livingston trembled for hours in pure indignation. The gardenias, as you might expect, are on the liberal side. When one of them started gloating about Fritz Mondale, and how the Vice President would rally a liberal Senate, I picked up a pair of heavy clippers. "If you don't shut up," I said, "I'm going to prune your two top branches." The gardenia started to cry. It's hard to reason with a weepy gardenia. "I was only kidding," I kept saying, but the gardenia would not be appeased. I don't get along too well with the fluffy ruffles, either, probably because it speaks only a fern language.

Backster and his fellow experimenters believe that some plants have enough electric potential to operate small switches on remote request. It also seems possible that plants, which cannot tell a lie, could be used as witnesses. Hook a polygraph to a philodendron, and old Silent Phil will tell you if the maid is swiping your gin.

Our neighbor Mrs. Carney, the colonel's wife, read the book, too. She is a no-nonsense gardener, and didn't know quite what to think of it. But on New Year's Day she transplanted a couple of pine trees, smacked the mounded earth with her spade, and looked the pine trees dead in the eye. "If you bums don't grow," she said, "I'll pull you up by the roots." Those proved to be pretty smart pine trees. They salute whenever Mrs. Carney walks by, and they've been growing superbly ever since. The Backster effect, as it is called, may not work for everybody, but in the Blue Ridge Mountains, where there's nobody much to talk to, a Republican rubber plant named Livingston is nice to have around.

One of the curious aspects of gardening is that most of the plants sound like awful diseases or Louisiana cooks. The thought recurs every January, when the catalog comes in from White Flower Farm in Litchfield, Connecticut. I digress long enough to suggest that any gardener who hasn't discovered the White Flower Farm Catalog has missed the most delightful garden publication of them all. The principal editor, one "Amos Pettingill," goes at his descriptive tasks with love that has been tempered by a wry and tender humor. When some idea has flopped, such as the idea of putting lime around a clematis, he lets you know. We could have told him what does work for a clematis: two cups of wood ash.

It's the easiest thing on earth, thumbing through a flower catalog, to become enchanted with the names. Anyone who has lived in the South has encountered a kitchen genius by the name of Lobelia or Begonia or Veronica or Dianthus. Or how about Aperula and Buddleia? As for diseases, I would as soon forget amsonia and artemisia, but euphoria is nice to remember. At the thought of epimedium, I itch; at the prospect of plumbago, I ache. There's coreopsis, gloxinia, and physostegia. How would you like a bad case of lasiocarpa compacta? When we were doing some landscaping a few years ago, Marie wanted a *Picea pungens glauca pendula*. It's a handsome spruce, but I wouldn't have felt comfortable with it.

During the years we lived in Richmond, our gardening instincts were severely curbed. The Hanover Avenue townhouse had a small brick patio in back. Around the edges, next to the wall, ran a border maybe 30 inches wide. The border swiftly filled with camellias, azaleas, and ilex Helleri — and that was it. There was no room for anything else.

Then came the Grand Remove to Rappahannock, and suddenly we had acres and acres. I have to be cautious with that first person plural. Early on I discovered that the best of all ways for a sedentary man to find pleasure in the glories of gardening is to find pleasure in the glories of his wife's gardening. This relieves him of both responsibility and labor, but permits him to share equally in the harvest. If a man is sufficiently ignorant of the difference beween weeds on the one hand, and plants and flowers on the other, and if he commits a couple of disastrous errors at the outset— pulling up the thyme, for example, under the impression that he is helpfully pulling up chickweed — he may never be permitted to weed a garden at all. Marie has the green and dirty thumb. She works; and I admire.

We became nuts, in a modest way, on this business of organic gardening. To skeptics who insist it is impossible to get along without dusts and sprays and pesticides and commercial fertilizers, I say simply, for the record, organic gardening *works*. It truly does. All that is required is that one accept an abiding commitment, to paraphrase the Prayer Book, to the earth: All things come of thee, O Soil, and of thine own have we given thee. Of course you have to work at the project.

Almost the first thing we built, after the Grand Remove, was the compost pen — a 6 x 6 depository, fenced in chicken wire five feet high. The first piece of farm equipment was a noisy little shredder and mulcher, known as the gloppity-glop machine. This one came from Sears, and performed splendidly until it finally wore out. Then we acquired a sturdy monster from the W-W people in Wichita, and it has proved magnificent; it swallows anything you toss down its hungry gullet and begs for more besides.

Into the compost pen we mounded up grass cuttings, shredded leaves, cornstalks, dead flowers, plain weeds, and kitchen garbage. Anything! An occasional seasoning with dried meadow muffins improves the mix. We used to go marching across the Burke pastures, she with a small shovel and I with a green plastic bag, foraging for these remarkable objects. "There's a great one!" I would cry. "Here's a beauty," she would say. Passersby on the Woodville road observed our procession with incredulity and amazement; they thought we were mad.

But the compost mounted up, rich beyond the dreams of J. Paul Getty, and goodness knows we needed it. I have alluded to the rocks of Rockyhannock County, but perhaps I have not dwelled sufficiently upon the characteristics of the soil. The characteristics of the soil are as follows: brick clay. Try to plant a tree some time. The ground is a shovel-breaker and a hoe-snapper. You come up with clods as hard as billiard balls. But once a few cartloads of compost have been dug in, a garden plot begins to smile, and curtsey, and make its manners; it begins to loosen up, and after a while the earthworms appear. One of these days, so help me, I shall compose an Ode to the Earthworm. Hail to thee, O Worm! If you talk gently to the worms, they will work all day and all night for you and never ask for a raise in pay.

In the summer of 1970, after the new house was built, we bought some 2 x 6 planks in 12-foot lengths. Against the advice of *Organic Gardening* magazine, which is generally sound but no more infallible than the rest of the press, we coated the planks with creosote. The magazine says that creosote will shrivel every tender root that comes in contact with it, but don't you believe it. We built half a dozen frames in the ground, each 6 x 12 feet, and another long frame 6 x 27 feet toward the bottom of a terraced slope, and we heaped them knee-deep in compost. It wasn't exactly a Virginia plantation, but it was the next best thing. Later we enlarged the garden with a 12 x 12 box for corn and a couple of 4 x 8's. The advantages of such a garden arrangement are partly practical and partly psychological. You can reach any part of the box with a rake or hoe, and when it comes to planting, or weeding, or picking, there's a terminal point in sight. You don't get discouraged. Besides, when the in-between grass paths are trimmed, they look pretty.

In such boxes, with minimal effort, enormous pleasure, and modest profit, we grow enough vegetables to feed a small army. In summer that is the number of houseguests we get. Tomatoes, onions, carrots, radishes, cucumbers, squashes, corn, okra, broccoli, snowpeas, June peas, baby limas, snap beans, dill, cantaloupes, asparagus — it is hard to remember them all. Something in the composition of the soil appears to be pure heaven for zucchini. Once the zucchini begin to grow, there is no stopping them. In the morning you notice a blossom; by afternoon a four-inch marvel has appeared; a day or so later, if you forget to pick, the thing is as big as a Smithfield ham. We have grown zucchinis half the size of grand pianos. It takes two men and a pickup truck to move them.

Most of the produce gets eaten right away. Permit me an observation on the matter of corn. Somewhere, long ago, I read the findings of an agronomist to this effect — that corn loses half its flavor within 10 minutes after it is picked and shucked, half of what is left within an hour, and half of what remains in the next 24 hours. I believe this to be true. The way to prepare corn on the cob is to put a kettle of lightly salted water on to boil, and to get all the rest of the meal done first — the table set, the butter softened, the salt and pepper at the ready, hands washed, milk poured, everything poised. Then you go to the garden—six or eight hands are better than two— and you pick a dozen ears. You shuck them on the spot, and as fast as a granddaughter's legs can run you hustle those golden jewels to the pot. Three minutes! No more! And that, my brothers and sisters, is corn on the cob. Subsequently, of course, you feed the cobs to the gloppity-glop machine, and it all begins anew.

The produce that isn't consumed on the spot is diverted to the making of pickles, relishes, chutney, and soup to go in the freezer. This is a ritual act, performed with love and grace whenever August rolls around. We go to the garden in the cool of the early morning, with the two collies trotting along to supervise, and we pick for half an hour or so — cucumbers, zucchini, tomatoes, okra, snap beans, whatever is ready to be picked. The pleasure never palls. Marveling, we harvest in summer the dreams of winter and the hopes of spring.

A few hours later the gleaming jars stand in stunning array. Messrs. Tiffany and Cartier never displayed anything more brilliant in their Fifth Avenue castles — relishes of rubies, pickles of jade, peaches of amber. The kitchen is redolent of vinegar, garlic, spices, dill, of herbs fresh picked, the fragrances of home. The pantry shelves are showcases of topaz, tourmaline, and emeralds. The women's libbers will never understand the proposition, or accept it, but it is as important to a countrywoman to pickle as it is important to a countryman to get in the firewood. One measures fulfillment in pints, quarts, and split oak logs.

The perceptive observer will note that I have had nothing to say, thus far, of the black-eyed pea. This is not by accident, but by design. It is a saving of the best for last. I should like to say a great deal of the black-eyed pea, but ten thousand words of praise would not amount to a *great deal*. The topic is inexhaustible. It is impossible sufficiently to laud the Noble Legume.

In the years before I left Richmond, I served — and served with some dignity and distinction, I may add — as Founding Father of the Black-Eyed Pea Society of America. Faithful to the democratic tradition that characterizes the great trade unions and bar associations, I elected myself Number One Pea, Pro Tempore, and because I have continued to appoint the Society's nonexistent nominating committee, I have occupied that exalted office without successful challenge from that day to this. I drafted the Society's simple constitution; I wrote the words and music of its stirring marching song; I designed the crest and coat of arms. These are among the proudest accomplishments of a career that otherwise might have been wholly without an achievement worth mentioning.

I am often asked, in my capacity as Number One Pea, Pro Tem., if the black-eyed pea is soul food. Yes, of course it is soul food. It is good not only for the soul, but for the heart, mind, the liver, the gizzard, the forehand and the backhand as well.

Occasionally, though seldom in my presence, people scorn the Noble Legume as a mere cowpea, suitable only for the lower classes. This is nonsense. The black-eyed pea is above social status. It is also below social status. It sustains both commoner and king. Every President of the United States since Rutherford B. Hayes, with the sole exception of Mr. Harding, is known to have relished the black-eyed pea. It is the favorite food of second basemen, public auditors, gas inspectors and masters of the flugelhorn.

Black-eyed peas are of ancient origin. In its dried form, the black-eyed pea traveled with Moses in the wilderness; there is high authority, indeed, for the proposition that this is the manna described in Exodus 16. The black-eyed pea is known to have sustained Alexander; it also sustained Pericles; it did no harm to Julius Caesar. The black-eyed pea came to Virginia with John Smith in 1607; it has been the vegetable of choice in our great houses ever since.

Dr. George Bagby, a venerable Lynchburg editor of the 19th Century, once delivered himself a few modest words of praise for the Noble Legume.

"As an edible," Dr. Bagby declared, "the vegetable has not its equal. It is good for man or beast. It is the concentrated quintessence of the delightful. It is harmless. It may be eaten in any quantity. It is hard to quit eating it. It does you good all over. Its taste is indescribably delicious. In brief, it is meat, drink, lodging, house rent, taxes, and a free ticket to the fair and back again. Blessed pea! Sublime pellet! Celestial molecule! Divine little gob! All that Virginia is, or has been or can be, is owed to thee."

Such temperate understatement has for many years distinguished Southern journalism. Prior to the late War for Southern Independence, an aspiring young journalist, eager to get into editorial writing, was examined by his elders in Latin, Greek, and the Convention of 1787. After Appomattox, the custom was to question the applicant on the commanders at Shiloh, down to the rank of major, on both sides. Most of this scholarship has gone by the boards in our own permissive time, but one requirement remains. The categorical imperative is that a Virginia editor must eat black-eyed peas not less frequently than three times a week; and he must give every appearance of liking them. When he travels abroad in the land, to Charleston, Savannah, and Fort Worth, he must defend the black-eyed pea against the inferior gastronomic claims of she-crab soup, hominy grits, and five-alarm chili. When a Virginia editor goes on vacation, he is expected to spend his days chiefly in contemplation of the black-eyed pea.

No Virginia editor ever has been known to spend his vacation otherwise. From these salubrious reflections there emerges the sterling character of our editorial pages.

From these modest observations, you will surmise that black-eyed peas were the first crop to be planted at White Walnut Hill, and your surmise would be precisely on target. Imagine, if you will, the perfection of an August afternoon. The husbandman and his wife proceed to the pea patch about 15 minutes before drinking time. There they pick a peck of black-eyed peas. The jade pods are somewhat larger than a good copy pencil; they dangle from the lush vines like tassels on a lampshade. This splendid harvest then is taken to a back porch, where the jeweled peas are popped from their velvet encasements. Thence to the stove, where a kettle of fresh tomatoes has been simmering, smershed in happy communion with celery, onions, and bits of crisp bacon, salt, pepper, cayenne and Tabasco. The black-eyed peas then are cooked by themselves, with a hefty wedge of fatback, or added to the tomatoes. The better form is to cook them solo and to serve them beside the tomatoes with a slab of hot corn bread.

But it is among the infinite glories of the Noble Legume that it cannot be cooked badly. The black-eyed pea is good the next day. It is good the day after that. The black-eyed pea may be squashed, mashed, pureed, mixed with rice, or fried in the form of patties, hash, or petits fours. Down in Athens, Texas, in 1973, the annual black-eyed pea jamboree saw first prize awarded to a gentlewoman who concocted a black-eyed pea mousse. No other vegetable can make that claim. No other vegetable can even approach it.

Reading this over, I am struck with the thought that I have often touched upon the colors of our mountain life. This is perhaps because I have lived so long with Marie, sculptor and painter, to whom color is so important. She sees the yellows of the hills in early spring, before they have tended toward the greens, and says, "These are not the yellows of Florence." She looks intently at the green of the chestnut oak in midsummer and thinks, "This is not quite the green of Corsica in fall." All our seasons come in color combinations. Winter is the time of black and white; spring is grass green and blossom pink; summer is heavy green, burnt umber. Autumn is the red and golden season, and after the pickling is done, autumn is upon us. Toward the end of September, we remark, these old and comfortable mountains will soon be at their peak of color. One chilling frost will turn the oaks, and overnight the tapestry will be complete. Already, we say, the hills are wrapped in Oriental rugs, woven in a warp of evergreen. The pines, cedars, spruce and firs are conservatives in this crowd; they never change.

The glory of these mountains is that hardwoods and soft are mixed together. The dogwoods are like teen-aged daughters: They cannot wait. One afternoon the big dogwood on the knoll is a sober, respectable green. The next morning it is cheerleader red, waving its arms for attention and calling, oh, look at me, look at me!

In summer the sumac is an ordinary bush. You never notice it twice. In early October its blood red stems are flying crimson pennants, wind-whipped, dark-speckled. The motherly old chestnut has turned to dull yellow. The poison oak vines are cordovan brown and oxblood red, white-ribbed, fish-boned, their toxic qualities now quite concealed. On every slope, the gums shed their shiny leather leaves, soft as calfskin, soft as slippers. The poplars are pure gold — gold as newly minted medallions for some commemorative affair — and the maples turn to scarlet guardsmen on parade.

What we witness in September, I submit, is a turn in the cycle of death and renewal. Autumn is end and beginning. The leaves fall, sifting gently down, but the seeds fall with them, and the forest floor is a mass of nuts, berries, pods—the motionless and imperceptible germs of life unborn. There never is time to pick all the apples; our orchards are carpeted with windfalls, the fruit rotting, the seeds returning, the last of the insects gorging themselves on the yielding flesh.

The garden is done for, the cornstalks forlorn as old soldiers, standing around, waiting for orders. The cucumbers are swollen yellow, the orderly rows of beans a mass of weeds. Now the cantaloupes are gone, but a few melons survive — those the groundhogs haven't assaulted — and the pumpkins slowly turn to burnished copper pots. We note, in such a September, that a deer has been sleeping in the squash beds — a lumpy place for bedding — and a fraternity of rabbits has been holding a rowdy convention by the fencerow.

Gently, day by day, we lapse at summer's end into the preparing time. For the prudent husbandman, it is the firewood time; this is a chore that is always put off for much too long. But it has to be done; and some of life's satisfactions, one reflects, come remarkably cheap. If you hit a fire log just right, with a good sharp splitting maul, the log splits clean, halves clean, quarters clean, and the kindling piles up. I do not wonder that Bismarck, toward the end of his life, made a reputation splitting logs. Order, and usefulness, and fulfilled necessity — these are no bad things.

The burnt umber days of August and September mean long shadows in the afternoon. The golden days grow short. The mornings of October are often dark and broody, fog hugging the hollows, but the nights are cold and apple-crisp, and the fallow fields are luminous beneath a harvest moon. Back in 1967, when we were still camping out in the old Corbin cottage, I wrote of such a night. The oldest boy had stepped outside to feed Lorenzo, then a collie puppy. The oldest boy cried: "Come look!"

A spider was weaving a geodetic web between two posts of the porch, spinning spirals around a score of radials as nimbly as a guitarist working on his frets. The youngest boy was dispatched to fetch the spider book — youngest boys expect this sort of thing — and there followed a heads-together flipping of pages. It was a spider from the family *Epeiridae,* we concluded, probably *E. sclopetaria.*

For nearly an hour we watched this tireless Arachne construct her two-foot trap, picking her way from strand to strand, never pausing, leaving a moonlit trail of new-spun web behind. The youngest boy caught a tiny moth and tossed it in. The moth fluttered, struggled; but in one headlong plunge the spider was upon it, wrapping a shroud around her unexpected prey. Then back to work, until the web became a silver diadem, intricate as a snowflake, a work of perfect beauty on a country porch. And as the moon passed by, the mist came up; the web shimmered, delicate and deadly, glistening with danger.

The next morning, alas, the web was a dull grey, tattered from the lilliputian struggles of the night. The lady of the house, swinging an energetic broom, wrote the inevitable ending to ephemeral loveliness. "Another durned cobweb," she said, as ladies of the house have always said; and she swung mightily. A philosopher might have reflected that Epicurus had the right idea. Savor a moment of beauty while you can. Tonight Arachne weaves her tapestry by moonlight; tomorrow comes the broom.

These are meditations for a summer's end. They emerge from that keen awareness of time, that rhythm of the seasons, which keeps its steady beat in the rural heart. Men say of the factory and the office that a great many days seem "just the same," that "nothing different ever happens." And this is true, of course, of life in farming country. Yet there is always that rhythm, and it is always present. One is acutely conscious of the bursting seed, the nesting bird, the ripening fruit. Watermen will understand what I grope to say: They know when a tide will turn.

Here in the Blue Ridge, summer's end is a time for harvesting early apples, a time for cutting the last hay, a time for putting corn to silage. Across the nation, farmers in other areas can substitute their own chronology. On every farm it is constantly a time for something. We awake now and then to the distant snarl of power saws: It is firewood time. Already the nights are cold. The ponds at dawn give off the pale gray breath of autumn just ahead.

It is not only the sense of time that casts a spell upon the countryside. There is also, I suspect, a sense of possession, a deep sense of place. Some of the great historians and psychoanalysts of the South—Cash, Percy, Woodward, Rubin—used to emphasize this aspect of the Southern character, and for a long time I supposed we Southerners had a monopoly on this primitive virtue. But it is not so. You hit the same love of place in the plainsman and the Yankee and the rancher.

To live in a great city has its good points, but a sense of permanence is not among them. A man may have pride, to be sure, in "my house" or "my apartment," but he knows an uneasy apprehension that by tomorrow it may be somebody else's shopping center. How many structures remain in Manhattan that one might have seen in that city a hundred years ago? Pitifully few, I suppose. But the countryman, scuffing his boots in the good earth, abides with hills that have been there forever. "My land," he says. "This is my place."

"Man is a social animal," said Spinoza, and no one doubts it. The country can be marvelously social when it pleases, as anyone will tell you who has just come from the Amissville fair. But at a deeper level, man is an antisocial animal also. Most of the tensions of the city are rooted in the ant-swarm crowd; one can be lonely in the city, but one is seldom, in any absolute sense, alone.

It is better here in the hills. Our stars are not so brilliant as those of Arizona, but they suffice. Here one knows space by night and day, the wind sweeping, the hawk gliding free in a smogless sky. Space, and place, and time—these three. One marks the summer's end; and one learns a countryman's lesson in the yellowing willow and the twilight's sudden, shivery chill: There is no end, and no beginning either.

Part Five

Containing a few random reflections
upon the loss of privacy, the sense of place,
the need for ritual, and the
nature of a grand design.

When we first came to Rappahannock County in 1966 and moved into the old Corbin cottage, we found something close to rapture in an experience that gets rarer all the time in American life. It is the experience of total privacy. From the crest of White Walnut Hill, not a single human habitation could be seen. By night, the only visible man-made light was by Mr. O'Bannon's barn a mile away. It was then possible, on the lilac mornings of spring, to step outside mother-naked, and to revel in the sensual touch of April all around you. On clear days you could look at Old Rag Mountain, 25 miles away, and be certain no one was looking at you.

In time this glorious privacy disappeared. Jimmy Falls built his bungalow on the crest of a hill to the north, and Tom Geoghegan built his cottage on a hill to the east, and modesty commanded that we go bathrobed into the April zephyrs. Even so, nothing changed in the basic quality of country life. It remained essentially private. Country people, in my observation, tend to mind their own business. As a general rule, they don't pry; they keep their curiosity in check; they gossip, of course, as all humans do, but they shun anything that might involve an intimate relationship. If Rappahannockers spoke French, you'd never hear the familiar *tu*. An arm's length, they figure, is about the right distance to be observed.

Elsewhere in the country, this sense of reserve is having a rocky time. The 60's and 70's may be remembered, in one sense, in terms of the chic exhortation of the time: Let it all hang out! Thomas J. Cottle, a social psychologist attached to the Children's Defense Fund in Cambridge, Massachusetts, described the movement succinctly in a magazine piece in the fall of 1975. A whole industry had grown up, he said, to teach the uptight folks to open up. The idea is "to pull those inner feelings out of ourselves, right up there in front for everyone to see. ... First go the clothes, then the easy feelings, then the tough feelings, then the real secrets, and finally the entire inner self. When all this stuff has been exposed, we will supposedly be free, or equal, or open, or renewed, or something."

Instead of letting it all hang out, Dr. Cottle urged a

countermovement: Let a little stay in. I'd vote for that. In a free society, of course, those who get their kicks from mutual self-revelation ought to be free to pursue their inquisitive hobbies. The psychological strip act, provided it's done voluntarily, is all right with me. Different strokes for different folks. But as Dr. Cottle pointed out in his article, an increasing number of children — and of adults also — have no option. They find themselves in situations where they are virtually compelled to turn over to strangers the keys to their closet doors.

"Some suburban public schools now have compulsory sensitivity groups for students as young as six; children are expected to reveal intimate feelings and their attitudes toward one another. In some of these programs children earn points for their team by expressing their feelings. Taciturn children run the risk of being criticized by their classmates for not playing the game, or being referred to the school psychologist as 'problems.' In certain school systems, school psychologists have begun diagnosing a new childhood disease called shyness. Students afflicted by this abnormality may receive drugs designed to 'open them up.'"

The more one learns of these trends, the more disturbing they seem. Some school administrators have set out systematically to preclude the possibility of privacy. Children in these advanced schools, as Dr. Cottle noted, no longer have desks or lockers of their own. In such schools, traditional course work yields to sensitivity training and to "psychological openness." Holding things in is dirty; letting them out is cleansing. By the time these students get to college, the notion of privacy has nearly disappeared. Everyone is urged to *communicate* with everyone else, to identify, to empathize, to relate. The gaping mouths of curiosity are fed by mutual regurgitation.

This same insatiable urge to explore can be observed widely in the everyday business of simply getting along. There is no refusing the census taker or the taxman. There is no way to open a charge account, or buy an insurance policy, or get a loan from the bank, or qualify for food stamps, or sign up for unemployment compensation, without disclosing personal information that winds up in some computer's memory bank, somewhere. The uneasy feeling can never be wholly suppressed that one's Social Security number opens the combination lock. Telephone records, bank records, school records, medical histories! It has become impossible, metaphorically speaking, to stand alone on a night-swept hill and see only the light of O'Bannon's barn.

To be sure, much of this incessant fact-gathering is both necessary and unavoidable. Some of the attitude-probing may have value to scholars and to personnel managers. In certain circumstances, candor can cleanse and confession can purge. But a vast deal of the fact-gathering serves no purpose except to keep the gatherers busy, and much of the psychological phlebotomy does more harm than good. I had a letter of outrage once from a parent out on the Pacific Coast. Her 10-year-old daughter had been required to fill out a long, inquisitive questionnaire. The school psychologist wanted to know: Do your mother and father sleep together?

If any such question ever were put to my granddaughter, I hope she would return a blunt reply: "This is none of your durned business. (Signed) Heather Elaine Kilpatrick." Growing up in rural Rappahannock County, where privacy still matters, I doubt that she will ever be asked.

Raising children is like rooting camellia crosses: You can know only generally, and never precisely, what you're going to get when the plant buds and blossoms. Watching a child grow is the most absorbing study I know of. Back in June of 1970 I wrote a piece that provoked a lively spate of mail.

This was summer break time in Rappahannock County, as it was across the land, and suddenly our place was swarming with young people returning from the college wars. It happens every June. These remarkably vigorous, athletic, supple creatures are done in by examinations, and done in by the rigors of the academic year, but not so done in that they cannot swim and play tennis all day and stay up eating and talking all night. They stay wound up; they never run down.

One of these flights of meadowlarks included a young lovely, aged 20, name of Lizbet, who had just finished her sophomore year at a Midwestern institution that had figured in the news of campus demonstrations. She was slim as a sixteenth note and clean as Sunday morning, with long dark hair and brown eyes the size of chocolate cookies.

"I see your column now and then," she began, "and I see you on TV, and I wanted to tell you I disagree with you all the way, I mean *all the way,* and I tell you this to your face because I think it's always better to say what you think, right out, you know, and not behind somebody's back, like, if you can't be honest, what've you got?"

I put a copy pencil in my book, marking the place, and asked mildly what had prompted this revelation. Before she could answer, it came to me: I had done a television commentary on student riots, mentioning her private college in passing, and I had delivered myself of a few steamy observations on student vandalism and violence.

"Look," Lizbet said, tossing her hair, "let me tell you how it is. It's prison, I mean, like being in prison, you can't talk to *anyone,* and the house rules, you know, are ridiculous — 12 o'clock curfew week-nights and only 1 A.M. on Fridays and Saturdays, and if you're going out of town you have to sign all these forms. You can't *imagine.* We're not children, you know.

"But it wasn't just the house rules. It was *everything,* you know, the food in the Union was terrible. I mean it was really greasy, and the student government was a farce, it was just meaningless, and nobody wanted to come back after Christmas."

Well, I asked, if she had known about the rules, and thought they were all that bad, why had she gone back a second year?

"You don't understand," she said. "After all, I mean we students are it. If we don't insist upon change, who will? But it wasn't just the rules and the food and all that, it was the big things—Nixon and Agnew, and this unjust immoral war, and half the professors in the Chem Lab are doing some kind of defense research, you know, and then Mr. Beasley got fired— he had been there four years, you know, *four years,* and fired, just like that."

"Ah," I said.

"He was the only good teacher they had. I had him for English Lit the first semester. I mean, he was sincere and dedicated and honest, and we'd talk about Vietnam and that corrupt puppet government they have—that creep, you know —and we'd write about injustice and human aspirations and all that, and he was relevant. Really, he was relevant. He made us *think.* Then it got out that his contract wasn't being re-newed, and that was it."

"Yes," I said.

"We had this big meeting at one of the boy's apartments, and we worked all one weekend on our manifesto, and I mean we worked on it. You said we were irresponsible. Listen. We talked over every one of our demands. We weren't radical. We wanted an end to the war, right now, and we all wanted justice for the black students, and the boys wanted ROTC abolished. The college has no right to let its professors help the govern-ment in defense research, so we wanted that stopped. We wanted Mr. Beasley rehired, and we demanded some reason-able changes in the dorm rules, and the bookstore, and the greasy food, and you know, things like that."

"Ummm," I said.

"And you know what?" she said. Her eyes flashed. "We had an orderly march to the president's office, and submitted our manifesto, and nothing happened. I mean *nothing hap-pened.* Oh, a committee was appointed, and the administra-tion said it welcomed *dialogue,* but nothing really happened. So some of the boys broke some windows at the ROTC build-ing. What else could they do? You know? And it was a few days after that when things got out of hand."

"Ah," I said, and just then Lizbet was summoned to go swimming. She departed in a swirl of dark hair, twitching her tennis racket, and I heard later on that she said Mr. Kilpatrick listened all right, "but I don't think I got through to him *at all.*"

Off and on during her junior year, Lizbet wrote me letters of passionate remonstrance and instruction, rifling her pages with exclamation points the size of baseball bats, but after a while she found me hopelessly unregenerate. In her senior year she worked as a volunteer in the McGovern campaign, and then something happened. I never knew exactly what. Love, perhaps. But she sent me an invitation to her graduation, with a note in bold black ink: "Do come! You'll love it! Peace!" A month later she was a ravishing bride in white dress and beaded train, coming down the aisle of a high fashion Episcopal church, and winking a happy wink as she passed me by.

It occurred to me at the time that what Lizbet had discovered was not only love but also, just possibly, the value of ritual, the worth of tradition. By the time she got to Commencement Week, the midnight curfews and the greasy food had faded into insignificance. She wouldn't have missed Graduation Day for the world. I hope she remembers the occasion five or ten years later, but I tend to doubt it.

It is a declining tradition, I am told, and it seems a pity to see the old rituals slip slowly away. At many colleges and universities, Commencement Week has been compressed to half a day. The administrations, yielding to the new permissiveness, permit the graduates to show up or stay away as they please; and many of the seniors, perceiving that commencement has been thus downgraded, save the gown rental money and take to their heels.

Baccalaureate sermons, I am further advised, are very nearly a thing of the past. State-supported institutions abandoned such ceremonies long ago, for fear such entanglement of church and state might result in the loss of Federal aid, and the custom falters even in private schools within the Bible belt. A number of colleges have ditched commencement speakers also, on the advice of student leaders threatening boycott or riot if they should be compelled to pretend attentiveness to one more adult voice. It is only a matter of time, perhaps, before the whole business is turned over to computers, and graduates receive not diplomas but printouts.

For some years, the last two weeks of May and the first two weeks of June found me on the commencement trail. I am out of the business now and seek no invitations. Of all the contemporary forms of oratory, the Commencement Address offers the most difficult challenge to the forensic art. Even the briefest address is too long. The sweating graduates, dabbing at their brows, do not want to be inspired. They want to be free. Their minds are fixed on a good cold beer. Or on other pleasures. Yet they endure the ceremony because many of them inchoately sense what I think Lizbet sensed — and that is the value, even the necessity, of formality in a society that is getting a little too shirt-sleeved for its own good. When we deny ceremony, we deny memory; we pull up roots.

The Roman Church in recent years has been going through this modernization process, yanking Greek and Latin from its mass; and with deference to the reverend fathers, I wonder if the "comprehension" and "participation" they have gained is half so useful as the mystery they have tossed away. The Episcopal Church is committed to the same folly; in their clumsy efforts to "improve" the Book of Common Prayer, a gang of clerical vandals have laid rude hands upon one of the great works of English literature. Doubtless their intentions are good, but so were the intentions of the March Hare when he buttered the Mad Hatter's watch.

The Latin of the Catholic mass once echoed a continuum of centuries; it proclaimed a universality of Catholics in all countries. The reformers objected that people could not understand the Latin, but this was odd because the parishioner with a missal had a translation right in front of his nose. It was objected further that the old rubrics contributed to a sense of remoteness, but I never could appreciate this objection either. Something is fundamentally wrong, it seems to me, in the notion that we ought to be palsy-walsy with God. O

146

Lord, Good Buddy, scrub our sins, okay? Amen, and Ten-Four. My own thought is that the Rappahannocker's rule should apply: Let us keep a respectful arm's length from divine power. And if we cannot exactly understand the old poetry, whether in Latin or in English, let us remember the observation of Coleridge that poetry gives most pleasure when only generally and not perfectly understood.

Mystery, tradition, hierarchy, authority, solemnity — all these have value. It is stupid to let them slip away. The British understand these things far better than we do. Viewed rationally, the tie-wigs of their judges and barristers are the merest frippery. The House of Commons could dispense with the costumed procession that brings the Speaker and the mace-bearer through Westminster's arching halls. What value inheres in royal ermine in an age of stainless steel?

It is the value of memory, the affirmation of a past, the recognition of rank and order. There is something in the uneasy, apprehensive soul of man that needs an occasional grand occasion. My friend Lizbet would have been just as validly married if she and Douglas had gotten into blue jeans and sweat shirts and slipped off to City Hall, but ritual would have been poorly served. A military post could function without reveille in the morning and taps at night, but we would lose that umbilical tie to bugles past.

The young people who scoff at commencement exercises put too much stock in being rational. They complain of the academic gowns, the tassels and the mortarboards, the speeches and sermons, and they object that these have nothing to do with education. Why award a diploma "magna cum laude" in a school where Latin no longer is taught?

The answer is that rationality ought never to be regarded as the be-all and end-all. The custom that seems meaningless has meaning in the fact that it is a custom. The man who gets into white tie, or into the regalia of the fraternal Moose, is not the same man one meets on the sidewalk at noon. He has embraced ritual; he is a little more elegant; he rises to meet an occasion. I said that I doubted Lizbet would remember her commencement speaker or recall one word that he said, and this is true of speakers and graduates generally. The words blow away on an evening breeze. But if the speeches are happily lost, the graduates may retain something else. Years hence they may recall the walk across a college or a high school stage, the milk-warm night, the flashbulbs like heat lightning on the steps outside. They will have known a little of pomp and circumstance. It is no bad thing to tuck away in tissue paper in the attics of the mind.

This is the way with the good memories. We store them. We put them invisibly in albums, like baby pictures or vacation snapshots, and now and then we turn the pages. The good memories are memories of people — of friends, families, lovers, children — but they also are memories of place. Even in our own restless time, when a fifth of the population moves somewhere every year, a sense of place endures; and it leaves, however faintly, a stamp upon our people.

Lawrence Durrell once wrote of this. "As you get to know Europe slowly," he said, "tasting the wines, cheeses and characters of the different countries, you begin to realize that the important determinant of any culture is after all — the spirit of the place. Just as one particular vineyard will always give you a special wine with discernible characteristics, so a Spain, an Italy, a Greece will always give you the same type of culture—will express itself through the human being just as it does through its wild flowers."

Durrell continues: "I don't believe the British character, for example, or the German has changed a lot since Tacitus first described it, and so long as people keep getting born Greek or French or Italian their culture-productions will bear the unmistakable signature of the place."

Durrell has a great gift of perceptive observation. Doubtless what he says of Europe is still generally true. Yet I suspect the "signature of the place" is fading, and the stamp of a nation or a region is no longer so sharply defined. Here in the United States, every generation loses a little diversity, a little of its distinctive flavor. The process is a slow dissolve, but it plainly is going forward. The regional wines lose their bouquet.

I speak of the process with regret. Once the American South had a culture—a character—as distinctive in its sharp variety as the culture of Italy or Great Britain. Within the South there were many Souths, black and white, town and country, Tidewater and Piedmont and Tennessee mountain. There never was a single "Southern accent." There were dozens. Touches of the Elizabethan tongue survived on Tangier Island off the Virginia coast. You could hear the Gullah dialect spoken in Summerfield, South Carolina. The children of Charleston played abauoot the haouoose. Back in 1941, as a young reporter, I wanted to mail a photograph and sought help from Miss Mary Traylor in the *News Leader*'s morgue. A venerable lady of indeterminate age, she resembled Poe's raven and was as fixed in her Richmond ways. She told me what I needed: A piece of cyorrugated cyardbo'd.

Most of these signatures of place have vanished now. When Jimmy Carter got himself elected President, half a dozen paperbacked manuals appeared, instructing a bemused public in how to speak Southern. These were good fun, but they were mostly sham. David Cohn once formulated Cohn's Law to determine the thickness of a Southern girl's Southern accent: The thickness increases by the square of the distance she travels north of the Mason-Dixon line. When Mr. Carter's Savannah ladies were campaigning for him in New Hampshire, you could bay-are-ly unduhstayand uh wuud they say-aid, but back home in Savannah they talked like everybody else. Once in Richmond I conducted a small competition to determine the closest phonetic spelling of the greetings that used to be exchanged between two Richmond girls who meet on the street. None of the entries hit it exactly. The first girl says, "Haiei, haou'r yew?" And the second says, "Ah'm fi-yine, haou'r yew?" You don't hear that much any more. Now they say, "What's up?", or "Hah ya doon?"

A few of the South's cities struggle to retain their identity, but the legions of highway engineers outnumber the antiquarian platoons. The old architecture goes down with the old elms. Even in the small towns, the courthouse squares sprout parking meters now. Midtown Atlanta is as glassy as Cleveland or Detroit. Something of the spirit survives—something of the Southerner's porch-swing patience—but a strong sense of community departs; it jets away from Charlotte on Eastern's nonstop to New York.

To be sure, one ought to guard against sentimentality about the good old days. The "spirit of place" had its limitations. The old New England character could be frost cold and granite hard. The prairies were wide, but they grew a narrowness of mind. Southern chivalry was lace on leg-irons.

Even so, the old stamps, the old signatures, had an irreplaceable value. It used to be possible to open the invisible album, and to hear in one's head genuinely different accents, to summon to mind distinctive architecture, to recall meals, restaurants, and hotels that exuded an honest sense of place. Now the suburbs of Savannah match the suburbs of Seattle. A traveler awakens in the Anywhere Motel; there is always the same Utrillo on the wall. And just across the street, McDonald's.

Even my beloved Rappahannock, immutable as it is, adapts to the inexorable trend. Back in the 1920's, the government established the Shenandoah National Park. Rangers, armed with eviction orders, sought to move the mountaineers away. A compassionate bureaucracy offered oil heat and inside plumbing in the valley down below. Bowing to superior force, the mountaineers moved out; but as soon as the rangers' backs were turned they came scrambling back to their cabins in the hills. They possessed a fierce spirit of place. Most of the old ones are dead now, and their children are eating store-bought Bar-B-Q in town. In the leaf-looking time, our highways swarm with tourists from St. Paul. They stop at roadside stands to buy the native crafts — the native crafts, that is to say, of Hong Kong, Taiwan, and Japan.

But I do not despair, and on my cheerful days I am persuaded that the dissolving process may not be so inevitable after all. The movement toward governmental regimentation has not peaked, but now and then it seems to be slowing. Many Americans are getting upset at the loss of privacy, and their number is growing. Coast to coast we still are fed the same daily diet of news—homogenized AP, capsulated Cronkite—but many newspapers and TV-radio stations are making an honest effort to devote better coverage to the local scene. A traveler encounters regional art shows that have, in fact, a regional character. The distinctively Southern novel is said to be undergoing renaissance. The signature of place is fading, but it may still be deciphered for a time.

We all of us have our blue and broody days, but if we have our wits about us we keep them in perspective. Rummaging through some old files, I came across the text of a lecture delivered some years ago at Westminster College in Missouri by C. P. Snow, the English philosopher, novelist and statesman. He was full of the terrible dark pessimism of age. This was his message:

"I have to say that I have been nearer to despair this year, 1968, than ever in my life."

Lord Snow had been driven to this despondency by his reflections upon the shortsightedness, stupidity, and selfishness of man. Looking to the future, he could see no hope that man would adopt effective measures of population control; he could see no prospect of new food supplies to ward off massive famine. These two ominous curves, he said, were on collision course. Human intelligence, if put to work, might yet prevent a collision. "But we have to take selfishness for granted." The probabilities, he thought, were that the rich would get richer and the poor poorer, until hunger created "suffering and desperation on a scale as yet unknown."

I first read Lord Snow's address on one of those pale golden afternoons that late November brings to the Blue Ridge. It must have been one of my blue and broody days, for the speech at first made a deep impression. I had lately been in Puerto

Rico, and there had been struck by the squalor of the barrios and the opulence of the glittering casinos. Lord Snow seemed to have it just about right. Then Marie and I went for a long walk in the woods in back of Colonel Carney's place, gathering pinecones to gild for the Thanksgiving table, and a few sprigs of holly to put above the cottage door. We spent an hour in the deep rustling silence of the woods; and I walked back ashamed. Ashamed, that is, of my first ill-considered notion to accept the awful forecast that Lord Snow propounded in Missouri. Probably he had his facts straight — the curve of population rising, the curve of food declining—but facts will not always lead a man to truth.

To yield to despair, it seems to me, is to fall into a form of blasphemy that should be pitied, not admired. I am no philosopher; I am a newspaperman, as skeptical as Lord Snow of the altruism of men and nations. I too have seen enough of selfishness to take selfishness for granted. Yet I believe that our universe was not contrived by accident, but by design; and I cannot conceive that this ordered design includes man's self-destruction.

This is not metaphysics. This is walking in the woods at dusk, inspecting in delight the jewelry of a holly leaf, looking beyond the slate mountains to a crescent moon and distant stars. To stand in this silence, to kneel on the forest floor and to marvel at a pinecone, is to sense the design. Man is part of it, the highest and most wonderful part of it; and the mind of man remains the greatest gift of all.

Oh, the mind of man is capable of pettiness, of self-deceit, of mulish stubbornness, of a blindness that will not see the needs of others. Who could deny it? Yet this precious instrument has brought us a long way from primeval darkness. The capacity is there, untouched, to straighten out and to separate the ominous curves Lord Snow deplored. We have only begun to harvest the bounty of the seas; the good earth retains untapped abundance. The intelligent inventiveness of man, by God's grace, has not failed us yet. Why should it fail in the next tick of eternity's clock?

So we came to the cottage that November evening, bringing firewood and holly leaves and pinecones, and bringing inarticulate thanks as well. It is too easy—it is no trick at all—to know gratitude for material things, the food we eat, the clothes we wear, the comforts that surround us. These come and go. They are matters of degree. It is the gift of the grand design that counts. Lord Snow was wrong. To despair is to abandon the plan, to shun the design; it is to believe in the inevitability of disorder. It is to confuse the tribulations of an hour, here and around the world, with the mute, enduring serenity of a pinecone sleeping on the forest floor.

Let me dwell for a moment on this business of thanksgiving. The holiday of the same name has lost much of its meaning, just as Christmas and Easter have lost most of theirs. It's a day off, the start of a long weekend, the beginning of the boom in retail sales. I wish we could bring the meaning back.

Except in election years, October ordinarily takes me abroad, to Europe or Africa or South America, and I come back to Rappahannock not long before Thanksgiving. The mind is overloaded with impressions that cannot be contained—the shanty slums above Caracas, the bullet eyes of a prime minister, the darkness of the Transkei, the silky smoothness of a Communist functionary in Milan. The spirit flags. But I pick up my car at the airport, and head west toward the mountains. The highway that leads me home has nothing much to offer for the first 50 miles, but just west of Amissville, where the new four lane section begins, an engineer with the soul of a poet has laid out a great climbing curve. At its crest the whole world opens. In one glorious burst of trumpets, the mountains fill the sky. And the bruised and weary heart gives grateful thanks.

Autumn then surrounds us. The old tapestries are hung, the Oriental rugs are spread upon the hills. By mid-November the reds are the reds of embers, not of fire. We have more of rusted iron and less of burnished gold. But here on this crest the spirit always lifts. One draws a long breath.

Do we, as Americans, ever truly reflect upon our blessings? Not often, I suspect. Do we understand—deeply understand—how fortunate we are? I doubt it. As a people, we are the biggest bellyachers on the face of the earth. We complain of racism, of discrimination, of rights unfulfilled; we complain of poverty, of ill housing, of traffic jams, of perfidy in public office; we are like the sophomore Lizbet, who with her fastidious sisters would march in ardent protest over greasy food. Well, I have seen Soweto, and had a meal in a Bantu hut, and smelled the stinks of Rio, and looked in the faces of Leningrad; and I have come home to the engineer's curve, and I have wept. I have wept.

It sounds a jarring note, I suppose, to quote Richard Nixon. I quote him anyhow. Time after time in the campaign of 1968, he used to wind up a speech with the same peroration. We reporters used to head for the bus when he reached the line. At the engineer's curve it comes back with overwhelming force: "If I could have chosen a time and a place to be born," Nixon would say, "I would have chosen the 20th Century in the United States of America."

I think he meant it. He was not speaking especially of our material wealth, of cattle in the fields, of orchards needlepointed on the hills, of skyscrapers, smokestacks, silos. For these material things we may indeed give thanks, and it is hypocritical to minimize their value. At any given time, yes, we may have millions out of work, and we too have wretched slums, and here in my own Rappahannock County, to get right down to it, 698 out of 2,024 housing units in 1970 "lacked some or all plumbing facilities." But in the general quality of their lives, Americans are incredibly better off than most of the people a reporter sees around the world.

The things of the spirit count for more. I coast in exultation down the long hill past the curve. Up ahead is little Washington, Virginia, and off to the right the white steeple of Trinity Church catches the sun's last shaft of light. There is the Courthouse, where lives the rule of law. And there is the

154

sheriff's office; he will not come at midnight pounding on my door. There is a polling place. There is the office of the Rappahannock *News,* there the library, there the public school.

The roads that I have followed around the world lead now to a graveled country lane, a bridge across White Walnut Run, a lamp in the window, a fire in the kitchen hearth. Home.

Once I returned from the road not long before Thanksgiving Day, a bleak and sullen day, the mountains shawled in mist. All the way home the radio had chattered of bad news. Thousands of miners were on strike, auto workers were idle, the cost of living was edging up, a crisis was promised in natural gas. This was three months after Nixon had resigned, and the stain of those sickening events had barely begun to fade. If some saccharine minister had urged us, on such an afternoon, to count our blessings, a sardonic voice would have asked: *What* blessings?

I went to the office to check the mail, turned on the lamps, and after a while the bitterness and the bad news slipped away. The office walls are lined with books. Here are the law books, row on row, red and khaki; they stand as straight as leathernecks on review. Here are the Annals of America, eagle-crested, bound in blue and gold. Here are the shelves on history and government, here the lives of famous men.

At such a time, in such a mood, one listens; and there is more to be heard than the wind piercing the storm windows, more than the bark of a dog outside. If one listens, the room fills with voices. These are the voices of Jamestown in the bitter winter of 1607; voices of Yorktown and of Valley Forge; voices that ring like great bronze bells. One has only to listen to hear young Tom Jefferson and old Ben Franklin, John Marshall laughing, John Randolph scolding, Abe Lincoln lifting his high-pitched voice above a crowd: "Our reliance is in the love of liberty which God has planted in us ..."

The imagination stirs. The books are clamoring to be heard. Here is the letter of a young soldier in the Revolution: "We seem always hungry, and most always wet, and by night chilled to the bone." The voices speak across regions and generations, soft voices from the South, hard voices from the West, Lee and Douglass side by side, soldier and slave together on a shelf, freed of the past. "I am as strong as a bull moose," cries Teddy Roosevelt. He speaks from a top shelf, next to old Mark Hanna. "You can use me to the limit!"

One listens, and rubs the worn volumes of history, coaxing the voices to speak out; and the voices speak of war, of depression, of the human struggle that won the West. They speak of slavery, dust bowls, soup lines, sweatshops, floods and earthquakes, of Presidents who lied. Look, they cry! America has known all this! And America has survived.

Do we hear these voices in November? Or do we hear only the ticking of a clock, the wind in the eaves, the creaking of a rafter? Is the American dream no more than that—a dream? We know better. It has all happened; it is all there to build on— the successes, the failures, the trial and errors, the good men and bad, the blood and tears and laughter.

Perhaps it is banal to say it, but it needs to be said. Politically, economically, and spiritually, for all its manifest shortcomings, our blessed land is the freest and strongest on earth. On a Thanksgiving Day in the Blue Ridge Mountains, or wherever Americans bow their heads, the prayer should rise not only from our lips but from our hearts — a prayer of thanks "for the return of seed-time and harvest, for the increase of the ground and the gathering-in of the fruits thereof, and for all the other blessings of thy merciful providence bestowed upon this nation and people." We ought to give thanks for what has been, and knowing that, for what will be.

Let me return to a theme I've touched upon before, the theme of the grand design. It is like a line of music; I cannot get it out of my head. To live in the mountains, close to the land and the animals, the birds and plants and insects, is to hear the theme all year. Its message is profoundly simple, and profoundly mysterious also: *Life goes on.* That is all there is to it. Everything that is, was; and everything that is, will be. On that slender premise whole theologies have been founded.

I am no preacher and was not meant to be. The metaphysics are beyond me. I am embarrassed to write of "God's presence." God is off my beat. But one autumn, not long after we came to Rappahannock County, I was walking across the yard on my way to the tool shed, and stooped down to pick up an acorn.

One acorn. There was nothing novel or distinctive about this nut-brown miracle. Thousands of acorns littered the grass. The acorn was clean, glossy, cool to the touch; the crested top was milled and knurled like the knob on a safe. I could not tell you what Saul of Tarsus encountered on that famous road to Damascus, when the light shone suddenly around him, but I know what he felt. He was trembling, and filled with astonishment, and so was I that afternoon. The great chestnut oak that towered above me had sprung from such an insignificant thing as this; and the oak contained within itself the generating power to seed whole forests, and the forests other forests. All was locked in this tiny, ingenious safe, the mystery, the glory, the wonder, and the grand design.

The overwhelming moment passed, but it returns. Once in the waiting time we were down on the hillside, pulling up briars and honeysuckle roots. It was February, but the frozen ground had thawed and we were eager to get at the earth. I dug with my hands through dry leaves, wet leaves, rotted leaves, and crumbling moldy bark. And behold: At the bottom of the dead, decaying mass a wild bulb was raising a green, impertinent shaft toward the unseen winter sun. I am not saying I found Divine Revelation. What I found, I think, was a wild iris.

The iris was not merely passively waiting; it was doing something more than surviving. It was growing, exactly according to plan, responding to rhythms and forces that were old before man was young. And it was drawing its own life from the dead leaves of long gone winters, from millennial maples and primeval oaks. I covered this unquenchable rhizome, patted it with a spade, and told it to be patient: March would come.

And that is part of this same unremarkable theme: March does come. And April. And in the garden of my wife the rue anemones come marching out, bright as toy soldiers on their parapets of stone. The dogwoods float in casual clouds among the hills; spring nestles in the drowsy hollows and laughs in the ripples of White Walnut Run.

This is the Resurrection time. Long before there was a Christian faith, as such, the humblest peasants recognized divinity in April: That which was dead, or so it must have seemed, had come to life again—the stiff branch, supple; the brown earth, green. This was the miracle: There is no death; there is in truth *eternal* life.

These are the simplest concepts of man's existence, and the most mysterious also. We know them as the "message of Easter," but it is a message that transcends the rites of any church or creed or organized religion. I would, if I could, invite skeptics to inspect our brave anemones; I would challenge doubting Thomases in my pea patch.

In a society surfeited with technological achievement, we are no longer easily amazed. We forget how to marvel; we are much too sophisticated to be struck dumb with wonder. The second moon walk was a bore. Foolishly we suppose that everything can be explained by "science." Given a telescope big enough, or a microscope strong enough, we perceive no secrets of galactic space or atomic particle that may not be revealed. Matter-of-factly we set our high school biologists to the task of dissecting an earthworm. We instruct them to report upon the nature of a worm. What they might perceive, if only they would look—if only they would look, and marvel, and wonder—is the nature of God instead.

These are lofty themes for a newspaperman. I cover politics, not ontology. But it is not required that one be learned in metaphysics to contemplate a pea patch. A rudimentary mastery of a shovel will suffice. Late in March we plunge shovels into the garden plot, turn under the dark compost, rake fine the crumbling clods, and press the inert seeds into orderly rows. These are the commonest routines, known to gardeners from time immemorial. Who could find excitement here?

But, look. The rain falls, and the sun warms, and something happens. It is the germination process. Germ of what? Germ of life, germ of Easter, germ inexplicable, germ of wonder. The dry seed ruptures and the green leaf uncurls. There is nothing phenomenal about it, but the botanists cannot explain it wholly.

It is not only the pea patch, of course, that yawns and stirs and nudges toward the sunlight. Down in the rock garden, where the rue anemones stand guard, a dozen tiny things come forth. A year or so ago, succumbing to the seductive allures of the White Flower Farm, we went grandly into heather. Over the winter it looked as if the grand investment had become a grand disaster. Nothing in the garden seemed deader than the heather. Now the tips are emerald, and the plants are coronets for fairy queens. Beneath a dogwood tree the sturdy hyacinths are soldier straight, their gaudy shakos on display. We have a marching band of tulips, forsythia as color guard. We have candytuft and coral bells, and a bumblebee as big as a blimp, floating over the whole parade.

"April is the cruellest month," wrote Eliot, "breeding lilacs out of the dead land, mixing memory and desire, stirring dull roots with spring rain." True enough, in its way. But April is the kindest month also. Here in the mountains, at least, it brings the blessed reassurance that life goes on, that death is no more than a passing season. The plan never falters; the design never changes. It is all ordered. It has all been *always* ordered.

Look to the rue anemone, if you will, or to the pea patch, or to the stubborn weed that thrusts its shoulders through a city street. This is how it was, is now, and ever shall be, the world without end. April is remembering, and Easter is knowing, and in the serene certainty of spring recurring, who can fear the distant fall?

Letters to Heather

I have here inserted the birthday letters to Heather, including a special letter at the time of her great-grandfather's death in the fall of 1974. This great-grandfather was Ben Pietri, Marie's father. As a newsman, I have met some remarkable people over the years — Presidents, Prime Ministers, authors, actors, financiers, miscellaneous heads of state — but in the *Reader's Digest* phrase, Ben was the most remarkable man I ever met. I wish Heather and the other grandchildren could have known him.

The birthday letters, as I have mentioned earlier, are included largely for the benefit of loving parents and fatuous grandpas who have daughters and granddaughters about the same age. The reader who is not so situated can skip them, or save them for the time when he may encounter a little girl who is two, three, four, five, or six. Having raised three sons, I can tell you that nothing quite matches having a Heather.

* * *

AT TWO, JULY 28, 1972

Dear Heather:

What, two already? How did you manage to grow so soon? It seems only yesterday — as a matter of fact, it was only yesterday—that your vocabulary began with "more milk" and ended with "bye-bye." And now you are talking like Bella Abzug. The next thing we know, you will be registering to vote. Two, eh? It is an elegant age.

Until this moment, according to custom in these matters, we had been calculating your maturity in months — 17 months, or 19 months, or whatever — which is a pretty silly way of going at it, especially for people like your grandfather who have trouble remembering how many months are in a year and can't subtract 12 from 19 without sober thought. Now, when we ask, how old is Heather, you cry "two!" and give us a V-for-victory sign, just like, if your McGovern-loving mother will forgive the words, Nixon saluting the hippies.

Two is the beginning of whole years for you, and perhaps the beginning of something else: Memory. We were wondering about it the other afternoon. You were climbing in and out of the blue plastic wading pool, stomping at the water to make it go splash, and catching the diamond drops in your hands. You were trotting about the yard, down to the rail fence and back, and you were discovering sun and shadow. You were as naked as a Botticelli cherub and as light as the breeze.

Will you remember? Will you remember how it was when you came on weekends here to White Walnut Hill, or to your Grandfather Stone's farm a few miles away? Will you remember the great oaks, the dark mountains, the green meadows rolling toward the sky? Will you remember when first you chased a firefly? Maybe not. It is a marvelous thing to be two, but remembering may have to wait.

But this much is clear, my naked friend: Two is a great time for talking, and talking is what you do best. You are your father's own child; and we know where he got the trait. You know, because we wrote them down on a tablet, a whole long list of lovely words: Arm, balloon, baby, ball, bath, bear, bed, beer, bird, bicycle, bib, brush, book, boot, boy, box, boat, bug, bunny, button, buckle, blue, and boom-boom, which is what the drum says.

You know: Cat, catch, cow, cookie, chair, cracker, cup, cheese, clothes, circle, candy, car, card, chicken, cheek, and of course you know Cyrano, your collie. You know: Did, doll, dog, down, donkey, door, do, drum, duck, David, daddy, dress, eye, ear, eight, eat, fine, fish, find, finger, flower, flag, food (you certainly know that one), foot, found, four, five, fan, frog.

You know: Go, girl, good, glass, green, hair, hand, happy, hat, head, hi, house, home, hear, hurt, honey, I, is, in, it, inside, ice, joy, juice, key, kiss, kitty, knee, leg, look, man, me, monkey, meow, moo, mess, milk, mouth, Michael, mommie, mouse, name, night-night, nose, no, nine, oval, open, outside, okay, one, pen, panties, parrot, please, puppy, potty, pocket, pool, and peep-peep, which is what the bird says.

You know: Quack-quack, ready, racket, snap, shoe, spoon, spank, sit down, square, stairs, steps, see, sock, swing, six, seven, sand, towel, thank you, tiger, turtle, train, triangle, tree, toes, two, this, three, ten, twenty, toot-toot, and T.V., which is where you picked up a lot of this baggage. You also know unh-unh, up, where, want, water, woman, wet, woof-woof, yes, zebra, zipper and zoom.

That is a pretty fair box of tools. And with every summer day that passes, you are learning to fashion ideas, to catch meaning like a firefly, to find delight in the spoken word that gives and receives. All this is fun for you, but ah, my small straw-blonde friend, you with the blue chicory eyes, you cannot imagine what fun it is to be the grandfather of a granddaughter, just turned two.

Love, My Love,
Grandfather

AT THREE, JULY 28, 1973

Dear Heather:

Three! You are honest and truly three years old today? I might have guessed two and a half, or two and three-quarters, but three? Why, it seems only day before yesterday, or maybe week before last, that you were honest and truly two. Heather, you are practically middle-aged.

A year ago, when you were honest and truly two, we were counting your vocabulary. You had picked up all kinds of strange and interesting words, but somehow they came out in very few sentences. Now you are talking not just in sentences, but in paragraphs, essays, and books.

You are turning into a talker, Heather, in the tradition of your great-great-Aunt Lucille. She laid down the family rule that in any given conversation, whenever the speaker takes a breath he loses the floor. Your father was in the direct line of her inheritance, and you take right after him.

In the past year, I rather regret to say, you have discovered the telephone. Not the play telephone. The real telephone. By next year, maybe you will learn that not all questions need to be answered, "I'm fine!" It is a little baffling, after all, when I ask, "Is your father there?", and you reply, "I'm fine."

You are discovering many other things also. You have discovered why people go to the bank: They go to the bank to get lollipops. And why do people go to the shoe store? They go to the shoe store to get a balloon. You are discovering the eternal truth that sandwiches taste better if they are cut into triangles instead of in squares. You are discovering colors — red, blue, purple, and polka dot.

Last year, learning the alphabet, you bogged down at G. This year you bog down at wubbiya. Your favorite book, at the moment, is the Sesame Street book, from which you have learned an imperishable assertion: "You're bananas!" You also have mastered, through the doubtful grace of your Uncle Kevin, "Go to the head of the class!"

What you have mainly learned in the past year, though, is how to be helpful. If you have a favorite sentence, this is it: "I want to help." So you help in weeding the garden, you help in shelling peas, you help in watering the lawn, you help in cleaning up the dishes, you help in making the beds, and now and then your mother wonders how in the world she ever got things done without your assistance. Mostly, however, she wonders how she ever gets things done with your assistance.

I like so many things about you it is hard to say what I like best. Maybe it is the way you bounce into a room. You come on like the happy princess in "Once Upon a Mattress," with your blue eyes shining and your blond hair flying, and you talk all in capital letters: "HI, GRANDFATHER! I'M FINE!" You sort of clear the air, Heather, like a small hurricane or a three-year-old typhoon. And when you let the collies in with you, barking and pawing and licking your face, the Marines, believe me, have landed.

But I think what I like even better is your lovely conception of time. Everything that has happened before, even if it happened five minutes ago, happened "yesterday." And everything that will happen hereafter, even if it is five minutes hence, will happen "tomorrow." Thus the yesterdays pile up very fast, and the tomorrows are all just ahead. You have your nose snubbed tight against the passing hour, and your world is pretty much bounded by lollipops yesterday and gumdrops tomorrow. When you are three years old, my small friend, that is not such a very bad world. It's a very good world.

One of these years, I doubtless will give you, because the books say I should, a vast deal of Very Sagacious Advice. Having been a newspaper editor, your grandfather is full of that. But at honest and truly three, a little advice will suffice: *Discover,* Heather, simply *discover!*

Discover the taste of rain, and the taste of mint, and the slippery feel of mud between your toes. Discover June bugs and fireflies and hummingbirds. Discover how the wind blows and a dog's tongue drips and the toad in the garden goes hop. Never stop discovering! And you will discover, a few tomorrows from today, the excitement of having a baby brother or sister who soon enough will discover, like you, how fine it is to be three.

I love you,
Grandfather K.

AT FOUR, JULY 28, 1974

Dear Heather:

Grandfather K., meaning me, had his own fourth birthday in the same week that saw Calvin Coolidge trounce John W. Davis. It must have been a turbulent time in our Oklahoma household, for my father — that would have been your great-grandfather — was supporting the Republican Coolidge and your great-great-uncles were voting for the Democrat Davis. Your great-great-grandfather, a Confederate captain, was down in Louisiana spinning in his grave.

Now you are having your fourth birthday in the midst of presidential earthquakes far more severe than those of 1924. I will tell you something: I do not remember one blessed thing about Coolidge, Davis, LaFollette, or for that matter, about the election of Herbert Hoover four years later. The first President I remember was Roosevelt, and the first political event I remember was Repeal. All this is over your head.

But it occurs to me that it is more of a blessing than a pity that you are likely to remember nothing at all about President Nixon, impeachment, and Watergate. If your memory is like mine, these events will wash over your recollection and leave no sediment behind. Years hence, when you read about Nixon, you will say, "Well, after all, I was only four that summer." It is a pretty good age to be in the summer of 1974.

The memories that we store up for you, and put away with your outgrown toys, are certain to be more pleasant than memories of a President at bay. If this past year has been a bad year for Presidents, it has been a great year for little girls.

This birthday, your fourth birthday, will be your first one at Hawthorn. Here you have your very own room, with big windows looking out at the Blue Ridge Mountains, and you have 500 acres, more or less, to run off your wiggles in. The old brick house was built about 1812, high on a hill that looks to everywhere, by a young doctor named Aylette Hawes who married a girl named Frances Thornton. A very long time after that, in 1961, your other grandfather—Grandfather Stone—bought the property and made it beautiful again. Now you are growing up in the hills and fields and ponds of Hawthorn, and these are the things you may remember.

You may remember a summer-soft evening in June, when you and your cousin Michael chased fireflies on the lawn. You were wearing a long dress, because it was a little cool that night, and you had to hitch up the dress with one hand and grab for light'nin bugs with the other. Michael caught all the fireflies, but he was a Southern gentleman: He let you put them in the Mason jar. You ran to and fro under the great maples for nearly an hour, until it got too dark to see, and then you let all the captive fireflies free "so they could go back home to their mommies and go to bed."

You may remember fishing with your father, sitting very still in the center of the canoe, not wiggling even a little bit, and most difficult of all, not even talking. You may remember the dark green iridescent fish, wet and shining; and the summer ducks that landed on the water; and the frogs that croaked by the banks.

You may remember the discovery of secret places on the farm—the cool sweet-sour smell of the barn, the empty horse stalls, the machine shop and tool shed, the hutches and pens where Grandfather Stone once raised pheasants and quail. You may remember discovering groundhogs and rabbits and chipmunks and a big black snake. You may remember squatting in the straw of the cow shed, your chicory-blue eyes big with amazement, watching a cow being milked.

Or perhaps we will remember all these things for you, and hold the memories in the warming ovens of our hearts: Heather learning to swim, Heather learning to "take turns," Heather holding a bottle for baby brother Douglas, Heather saying "good grief!" twenty times an hour. All this is Heather at four, and all this, my love, is happier to remember than to remember this summer as the summer they pinned Richard Nixon to the wall.

Grandfather

DEATH OF A GREAT-GRANDFATHER, OCTOBER 22, 1974

Dear Heather:

Your great-grandfather died a few days ago. You are four and he was 81, and it's not likely that you will retain much of a memory of him. That is a pity, for Ben Pietri was a remarkable man, and there are useful things to be learned from his life. He taught us, by his own example, that we can be whatever we truly want to be. He reminded us of the meaning of education and of the uses of curiosity. Until the very last months of his life, he never stopped learning and he never stopped looking. He was a great one for keeping his mouth shut.

Your great-grandfather was born in 1893, which will seem a very long time ago to you. The Civil War and Reconstruction had left his family quite poor. He dropped out of school when he was just a boy, and went to work repairing buggies. When automobiles came along, he fell in love with machines. He truly wanted to be a mechanic, so he made himself a master mechanic. He truly wanted to drive racing cars, so he learned to race on the dirt tracks of Virginia fairgrounds. He was barely five feet tall and had to be pillowed up to see where he was going, but he truly wanted to win—and he won.

Curiosity is a wonderful asset, Heather, and Ben had enough curiosity for ten men. He was always wondering how a thing worked, and whether it couldn't be made to work better. He would scratch his head and think, that if you tried this — and then this, and then this — maybe you could invent something new. When he was in his fifties he got fascinated with magnets, and he did things with magnets no one had ever thought of doing before.

You will never know anyone so curious. He was curious about bugs and plants and ferns and mosses. He was especially curious about fish. He spent so many hours fishing — just fishing, and watching, and keeping his mouth shut — that he came to understand how fish eat and sleep and swim around. He could cast a fly under a willow tree fifty feet away and never ruffle the water.

He was still working at 70, working with tools, designing and inventing, when calamity struck: His company told him he would have to retire. It was the worst thing that ever happened to him, to be told that he couldn't work any more. He went home to bed, pulled the covers over his head, and pronounced himself ready to die. After two days he couldn't stand it; and nobody could stand him either.

He got out of bed and started a whole new career. He truly wanted to be a sculptor, so he put his tools and his curiosity together and began making flowers and ferns and fountains of brass and steel and copper. This was part of the meaning of education. All those years in the woods and by the ponds, he had been learning. He had learned how a leaf is attached to the twig, and the twig to the branch, and the branch to the tree. He had learned how a grasshopper's legs fit together. He had seen the world in the eye of a frog.

This is knowledge, Heather — not book-knowledge, but knowledge-knowledge. To know how a leaf curls out of a bud is just as useful, in its way, as knowing how to write a sonnet, or build a bridge, or set a broken bone. Ben's copper leaves had the feeling of leaves because he had looked intently at leaves. Touch those leaves and you know all the autumns of his life.

At 80, he was still a colorful figure at the sidewalk art shows, joking with young artists, selling his flower sculptures, teasing about the blue ribbons he won. Then his health failed and his eyesight failed, and the heart that wouldn't give up, gave up. But life always goes on, Heather. You're learning that now, as a little girl growing up on a farm. The leaves of autumn do not die; they grow in another way in another spring. When you're a few years older, you'll be fishing too, on some perfectly perfect day when the fish are biting and the water sparkles. Think of your great-grandfather. Some part of him will still be there, still looking, still learning, still sharing the wonder of it all.

Grandfather

AT FIVE, JULY 28, 1975

Dear Heather:

Well, puddin', it's been quite a year for you — the year between four and five. One of these days we will have to sit down together and count the achievements.

Since your last birthday, you have learned to read, really-truly, at least a few words. You have learned to write your own name, in great sprawling capital letters that run uphill as if they were climbing a mountain. You have added at least a hundred million jillion words to your own vocabulary, and once you get wound up, your idea is to use them all at once. So much for book-learning.

What else? You've learned to swim, after a dog-paddle fashion. When it comes to flying a tricycle, you're ready to solo. You have had a go at your first fish, learned to sit in a canoe without wiggling, and just about stopped sucking your thumb. We were beginning to think you never would.

You have learned to tolerate, even to love, your two-year-old brother Douglas, and you do not even beat on him very hard. You no longer pick up the kitten by its neck. You have learned to gather cucumbers, snap beans and strawberries. You tie your own shoes and buckle your own seat belt.

That's a fine list for the year between four and five, but

what we've noticed, more than anything, is your growing independence. You're beginning to make up your own mind, rather than to have it made up for you. I have actually heard you say with my own ears, "I'm tired and want to go to sleep." A year ago you fought sleep as if it were spinach.

You may remember, later on, that this was the year your Aunt Lynn and Uncle Allen built their log house a quarter of a mile away. This was the way it was one afternoon, a week or so ago, when you decided to go over there and play.

You walked down the back kitchen steps of Hawthorn, saw a big bug at the bottom, and squatted down to have a closer look. The bug was a fuzzy orange caterpillar, and you had to let it crawl up your arm. Then you walked down the top of a stone wall, playing tightrope. You jumped off the wall, skinning your knee, and walked over a stump instead of around it. From the top of the stump, needless to say, you could see ever so much farther than from the ground. By this time Cyrano, the tricolor collie, was happily at your heels. The two of you marched down the road past the fishpond, past the work-shop, past the bird pens where your Grandfather Stone used to raise quail, past the tractor shed, and into the animal barn. There you said hello to the cow, scuffed up some straw, and threw a handful of hay in the air just to see how hay comes down.

From the barn you went past the apple orchard, and there Cyrano went into conniption fits of barking. It was a black snake, so you informed us later, at least tha-a-a-t long. Then you vanished into the woods, swinging on a vine, and after a while you tripped and fell over something, skinning the other knee. You came home bearing a broken bird's egg in a very grubby hand.

Maybe grubbiness goes with being five. For the Fourth of July your Aunt Lynn, bless her adventurous heart, provided a whole case of those ignitable, turny-twisty snakes, made in Taiwan, that fizz off with a smoke and a smell that are splendidly vile. The snakes disintegrate into soot and ash. One of these days, Heather, you will be 18, and clean and sweet-

171

smelling, and altogether lovely. On the Fourth of July 1975, you were a monumental mess.

It's much more important to remember these things, my love, than to remember that between four and five Mr. Nixon resigned his office, the economy went to the bow-wows, and the Americans and the Russians shook hands in space. Grown-ups will remember these events, because this is how grown-ups are. At five, it's far nicer to mark a birthday in terms of caterpillars, black snakes and bird's eggs, and to remember — to remember! — the wonder of it all.

Love,
Grandfather

AT SIX, JULY 28, 1976

Dear Heather:

Your sixth birthday is at hand. Our unmanned space vehicle has just landed successfully on Mars. Jimmy Carter has won the Democratic nomination for the presidency. That strikes me as a fair ranking of notable events in the order of their importance.

The Mars landing really is important, and the coming election has much meaning also. Come to think of it, if Mr. Carter wins in November, and gets reelected in 1980, you would be 14 before he left the White House. That's nothing very special for you to think about, but it is something for your Grandfather to think about. The thought makes him turn purple. Grandfathers look pretty funny that way.

But the truly important thing is being six. How about that! Some birthdays are better than others, and a sixth birthday comes first class. This is the birthday just before you go to school in September, when you will become a really-o, truly-o first-grader. That is ten times as much fun as being President.

Actually, you will be going back to school, for this summer finds you in a four-week "preschool experience" at Rappahannock County Elementary School. You have been catching the big yellow bus every morning at 8:20 and riding grandly back home a little after noon, and I asked you the other day how you liked the preschool experience and you said "guh-reat." That's the old affirmative outlook.

Thinking about that bus: Your Grandfather understands, from sources that cannot be revealed, that you raised so much ruckus in the back of the bus, bouncing up and down on the seat, that you have been summarily assigned to the front of the bus. Seat-bouncing is a no-no, but if that is the worst mischief you get into at six, we will be surprised.

This has been a good year, my love. You have grown up maybe two or three years in one. Last summer you were writing your name in large block letters that ran up a hill and slid back down again. Now you have your letters under re-markable control. Last summer you could hardly read at all. Now you are tackling all kinds of hard words, and because your parents are hipped on phonics, you are learning to sound-it-out, syl-la-ble by syl-la-ble. Before long I am going to get you on Con-sti-tu-tion, which is a nice grandfatherly word you ought to master soon.

In this past year you also have learned to swim like a guppy, though you still bellyflop something awful when you dive. You have been canoeing with your father on the Shenandoah. A couple of summers ago, the big discovery was fireflies. Now you're discovering the Big Dipper and the Evening Star—and Mars. You had your first experience with a curling iron the other day, when your Grandmother Honey went to work on your corn silk hair, and you emerged practically a little lady. "Guh-reat," you said.

Every day is discovery, which is as it should be, but this is mainly a time of human discovery — first of all of yourself, Heather Elaine of Hawthorn Farm, and secondly of other Heathers, and Billys, and Karens and Susans—and this has been a revelation to you after a life spent almost entirely with two cousins from the city, younger brother Douglas, and the Nicholson kids at the bottom of the hill. Other children! Twenty or thirty of them! White and black, and dumb and smart, and mean and nice, and all different! You are discover-ing the meaning of community, the first link on the chain to

173

the state, the nation, the world down here and the planets beyond.

Six will be a guh-reat year for you, Heather. You're learning not just letters and numbers and sounding out words. You're growing up. You're becoming your own person. A year ago all you wanted for your birthday was a frog and a couple of fishhooks. This year you want two hair ribbons and a Barbie Doll. You've come a long way, my love. And Happy Birthday!

Grandfather

AT SEVEN, JULY 28, 1977

Heather, my love:

Now and then, when we have nothing livelier to kick around, your grandmother and I do some wondering to this effect: We wonder what Heather, when she gets to be 57, will remember about Heather at seven. Probably not much; and this summer it's perhaps as well.

For this summer, the summer you are seven, has been a summer of disaster. It's been a bad year all the way around, but maybe if we put our minds to it, we'll learn something from the experience. Sweet are the uses of adversity! Mr. Shakespeare said that. You'll be encountering him before very long.

There were omens last fall. The great chestnut oak—that's the tree you and Douglas swing on—produced an astounding crop of acorns. We never had seen so many. They fell by the thousands, and all through November and December the squirrels were carting them away. We noticed that the collies had heavier undercoats than usual. The same thing was true of the rabbits and beavers and even the groundhogs. Their furs were remarkably thick. We noticed that some of the December birds, especially the grosbeaks, stayed for only a few days. Then they headed south.

Trees and birds and animals have a way of knowing things we don't know. In January, Rappahannock County was hit by four bitter weeks of pure ice. If it had been six feet of snow, it wouldn't have been so bad, for snow melts into the ground. The ice wouldn't melt. It just stayed there, and a freezing wind howled through the hollows and lashed the backs of our mountains. The cattle suffered, and the men suffered in getting hay to the herds. Some of the weaker calves froze to death.

The ice thawed finally, of course, and in March and April we began work on crops and gardens. The orchardists, having survived a miserable year in 1976, were hoping for a comeback in 1977. But you will discover, as a farm girl, how these things are. The sun beamed down in early April; the apples and peaches—foolish, frivolous trees!—burst into blossom two or three weeks early. And on May 10, wham! A killing frost and freeze almost wiped out the crop again.

Here at our place, we had maybe half an inch of rain in April, only a quarter-inch the whole month of May, and barely an inch in June. All the cycles of nature began to spin in reverse. For lack of snow, the ground water levels already were low; they dropped even lower. Wells and springs began to dry up. Streams stopped flowing. The old-timers said it was the worst drought since 1930.

I hope you won't remember how terrible this green country looked. The pastures were scorched, brown as toast, the brittle grass crunching under foot. The first cutting of hay was pathetic; for most farmers, there wasn't a second cutting. The cattle hurt their mouths grazing on the hard and barren land. At Madison and Front Royal, whole herds were sent to auction. So much hay had been fed in January that little remained in July. You could see the back of every barn in Rappahannock County.

For want of rain, the earthworms disappeared. For want of earthworms, the robins disappeared. Over at Hawthorn, you've always had purple martins; not this year. Usually we have bluebirds all summer; not this summer. The insect supply was down. Only a handful of Japanese beetles appeared to attack the grapes. The thermometer shot up to

100. And finally, officially, all this became a "disaster."

These are not very nice rememberings. Your grandfather has lots nicer ones: Heather learning really and truly to read; Heather writing her great-grandmother in Oklahoma; Heather swimming as effortlessly as a guppy in a tank; Heather trying on party clothes at a store in Charlottesville, and preening in the mirror; Heather delighting in a pocketbook of her own; Heather dabbing a dot of perfume behind her ear—and making a face, and laughing.

You grow in age and beauty, my love. You stand as straight as your canoe paddle; you're a little leggy and a little toothy, and you talk at five miles a minute as you always have. You can pick the ticks off a collie's back and squish 'em with a rock, all without blinking an eye, but you are all girl. You are not my tomboy Heather, but my granddaughter Heather. You are seven whole years old today, and you are loved. Never mind the disaster. You are loved. Remember that, and forget the scorched meadows and the stunted corn.

Grandfather

AT EIGHT, JULY 28, 1978

Heather, my love:

You know what you remind me of? You remind me of the wild chicory that every summer grows along our Blue Ridge Mountain roads. It grows tall and leggy and exuberantly, and it is topped by blue flowers that almost match the color of your eyes. Chicory is irrepressible, my love, and so are you.

This has been quite a year for you, the year between seven and eight. You have learned to read—really, truly read—and now you can read almost anything that comes along. You will read "exuberantly" in the first paragraph, sounding out the syllables one at a time, and when you have the word licked you will ask someone what it means. You have had an inquisitive cast of mind ever since you were in the two-year-old stage of "why?", and you seem to get more inquisitive all the time.

You also have learned to write, really to write, in whole sentences that are spelled correctly even if the penmanship is still a little wobbly. This summer, as part of your second-grade homework, you are keeping a journal of two sentences a day. I like some of your sentences better than some of mine: "We brought our dog Bess to a picnic. At the picnic everybody got wet." That tells the whole story. "I counted 30 strikes of lightning. Mike got bored." A strike of lightning is far superior to a stroke of lightning or a bolt of lightning.

For the record, I note that much of your summer journal deals with food. Are eight-year-old girls always hungry? I expect so. On the last day of camp, "we won the watermelon." On June 28, "I had a bubblegum ice cream." That is positively the most appalling thought your grandfather has had all day. "I made cookies with Linda." That is better. "We went blackberry picking." You did indeed, and you came home chigger-bit all over.

I saw nothing in your journal about the accident in June, when you cut your foot so badly on the backyard carousel, and maybe this was because you knew you were wrong and were ashamed to record the facts. You tried to stand in the middle of the turning mechanism, and you were lucky not to lose a foot. On July 6, "I got my stitches out." Okay. But it was a dumb thing you did.

Otherwise it was a happy year for you. You acquired a black Lab puppy, name of Bess. You found a snakeskin just after the snake had shed it—a perfect skin, head and eyes, still warm—and you and your father measured it with a carpenter's rule: Five feet, 10 inches. Some snake! You did your chores at the farm, and you did them happily. You got along better with younger brother Douglas, and you began to get little-girl conscious of how your hair looks and whether your dress is okay for church.

One evening a week or so ago, you came bursting into the kitchen, all flying legs and arms, to tell us about the canoe trip. You and Douglas and your father had gone up near Harpers Ferry, and stayed in a big orange tent full of chiggers, mosquitoes and spiders, and Saturday morning you took your position in the bow of the canoe, with Douglas in the middle and your father in the stern, and you headed down the Potomac.

"For a long time it was all flat water, all dull and plain and yucchy, but it was clean and we went swimming. Then about 2 o'clock we got to the White Horse Rapids, and that was great. One boat flipped over. Fourteen canoes gave up, but we kept on going. It was a little scary, but not much. Then we ran the Devil's Staircase. About 5 o'clock we pulled out of the river, and we ate hot dogs, spaghetti and baked beans. We slept in the big orange tent and Sunday morning we ran the Shenandoah—a mile of flat water and then Bull Falls! Wee!"

You told us all about it, with your eyes shining and your hands making white-water rapids in the air, and then you saw lightning bugs outside and ran out to catch a few in order to make a lantern from a Mason jar. These are nice things to remember. You are eight, Heather, and you are loved.

Grandfather

AT NINE, JULY 28, 1979

Heather, my love:

Nine? You are really and truly nine? It is not to be believed. Next year you will be 10; and into double digits. Then high school, college, job, marriage! It has been nice knowing you, Heather, and I thank you for pausing on the last plateau of little girlhood before ascending to the rarefied world of young ladies.

More than ever this summer, you remind me of the wild chicory that grows by our country roads. We call it a wildflower; most country people call it a weed. Anyhow, it grows tall and long and leggy, with blue-violet flowers at the top. If chicory only had freckles and a missing tooth, we could call it Heather instead.

I asked your father the other evening to tell me how you

were coming along with growing up, and he said that was the big thing between 8 and 9: You were truly growing up. You always have been willing to do the little chores around the farm, provided you were asked and directed. Now, he says, you see what has to be done—the table to be set, the dishes to be removed, the animals that have to be fed—and you do it. You almost never whine anymore; you sulk now and then, but not for long. Altogether, signs of progress are perceived.

I would add a genealogical observation of my own. (There is a hard word for you, but sound it out. Sound it out!) You have inherited the Kilpatrick talking gene. Your Grandfather Walker Stone was a fair enough talker in his strong, silent way, but he was positively mute compared to the talkers on your paternal side. We had so many non-stop, stem-winding talkers among my aunts and uncles that when they got together a parliamentary rule had to be established: Anyone who took a breath yielded the floor. Blood tells, Heather. Once you get started there's no stopping you.

You do have your quiet times, of course, when you complain pathetically that "there's nothing to do." The next time you inform me that such-and-such a thing is "BOR-ing," I swear I will pull your pigtails. At 9 years old, you ought not to pass a boring hour. Most of your quiet time is spent reading. Your father advises me, with a nice note of satisfaction in his voice, that you've become an absolute bookworm. You're also part tomboy and part pretty girl. More spice, I may add, than sugar.

A couple of months ago, when you came by our place after school, you left behind an English assignment in your third-grade classroom. Twenty declarative sentences. As I said last year, looking at your line-a-day diary, I like some of your sentences better than some of mine. Your grandfather tends to ramble. You knock your sentences off.

"On hot days we wade in the river." Years hence, that sentence may evoke all the beauty of the mountain land you live in—clear cold water spilling over the Rush River rapids, blue herons and goldfinches, eye of frog and mouth of fish, slippery rocks that are smooth to the touch.

"Flowers cover almost half our yard." They do, indeed, and your mother's vegetable gardens are equally extensive. You're absorbing the direct connection between the seed and the snap bean, the sowing and the reaping. "A butterfly settled on my finger." The essence of a summer afternoon cannot be captured more softly. You are discovering all kinds of wonderful things you have never observed so intently before. Toads hold no terror for you. You treat spiders with respect. You do not scream in the presence of a snake. It is an understanding butterfly that settles on your finger. Butterflies may know more than we think; this one knows a safe haven.

Someone asked you the other day how old you would be this month, and you said "Nine" with a world-weary sigh. I was reminded of the young lady in Memphis, just turned 25, who moaned pathetically that she was now "a quahtuh of a cintury old." There will be time enough to be weary 50 or 60 years down the road. In the summer of being 9-going-on-10, a whole drowsy world awakens at your touch.

Love,
Grandfather

AT TEN, JULY 28, 1980

Heather, my love:

I note for the record that you are about to become 10 years old. Very soon I will become 60 years old. We both will have reached nice round milestones along the road—you as a pre-teen, entitled to whatever privileges go with that delightful status, and I as a senior citizen entitled to a discount on my air fares. On the whole, this seems to me a nice arrangement. I have no interest in being 10 again, and you surely have no desire to be 60. Think of all the fun you would miss!

Further for the record: We stood you up against the kitchen door the other day, put a book on your head and marked the spot. Fifty-eight inches. This puts you only a couple of inches shy of your two grandmothers, and who knows where it will stop? You are growing like Alice when she ate the cake marked "Eat Me," and you would have very nice legs if they were not so chigger-bit. Country living, as we say.

On inspection I find you quite nice in other departments—nice eyes, blue as wildflowers; a good generous mouth; hair the color of mountain honey, usually in tangles, down to your shoulders. If you ever do anything drastic to that hair, besides combing it, I mean, I will strangle you with my bare hands. I hope you never mess with those freckles, either: signs of character. You know who you look like? A little like a young Sissy Spacek, the actress. Not beautiful, mind you, but good bones.

These descriptive memoranda are the least important. What pleases us more than anything is the clean, quick quality of your mind. You've matured phenomenally in the past year. You've sped past that Drew girl—what was her name, Nancy Drew—and you've swallowed *Little Women* whole. Like your mother and father, you have become an insatiable reader. Where's Heather? Got her nose in a book.

What else have you been up to? You're singing in the children's choir at Trinity Church, where you hit most of the notes right most of the time. You're big in the Girl Scouts, partly because of the 22 dozen Girl Scout cookies you pushed off on me. You swim like a minnow, and if you would only keep those legs together you might yet learn to dive. You go white-water canoeing with your father, handling your paddle with remarkable skill, and you don't flinch at cleaning a rabbit. Your grades in school are so-so.

I creep up delicately on this next observation, for it presents a delicate matter: I think you and I have grown much closer in the past year, and I love it. Two occasions will linger in my own memory, and I hope in yours.

One night the rest of them were tied up in a bridge game, and you and I started making music at the piano. We went through all the songs from *Sound of Music* and *The King and I*, me banging away and you singing, and when we finally gave up around 11 o'clock we kind of hugged each other. Grandfathers remember such things.

And one day last month, when you were visiting your Grandmother Stone in Washington, you met me for lunch at Jacqueline's on M Street. It's my favorite French restaurant in the city. You had arrived by cab a few minutes before I got there, as poised as a princess, and Jacques the senior waiter already had provided you with a cocktail: ginger ale, tinted pink with grenadine, with orange and cherry. It was one of the happiest luncheon dates I ever had. Before we left, you were working on "Merci, m'sieu," and "A bientot," and you were full of crab salad and Jacques' own stupendous serving of lime sherbet. You slept all the way back to Rappahannock County.

One of the great stars of musical comedy in my generation was a Frenchman, Maurice Chevalier. One of the songs that made him famous was called, *Thank Heaven for Little Girls.* He pronounced it "leetle gurlls," and he sang it with a twinkle. Watching you lately, I find that old song in my heart.

God bless, Heather. And happy 10th birthday.

Grandfather

AT ELEVEN, JULY 28, 1981

Heather, my love:

So we get to Milepost 11. It's what they used to call a way station, back in the days when passenger trains ran everywhere—a point that's neither here nor there, a kind of flag stop between little girl and young woman. It's not a bad place, just a necessary place, and I think you'll like it.

But, then, I can't think of anything offhand that you don't like, snakes and wasps and getting out of the swimming pool excepted. That's one of the truly nice things about you, Heather. You go at new experiences like you go to dinner, running hard for President of the Clean Plate Club. "That's neat," you say. In a disorderly world, what could be nicer?

For the record (your grandfather is forever saying, "for the record"), you reach 11 years old standing 4 feet, 10 inches tall and weighing just under 90 pounds. Your eyes get a little bluer year by year. That blond hair of yours comes down to your waist, and your legs stretch all the way to the floor. Those legs will be spectacular one of these days. Right now they're chigger-bit and blackberry-scratched, but that's country living.

It's been a good year for you, the year that you were 10. Back in October, you may remember, our house was open for the church's annual House Tour. You got assigned to serve as a hostess down at the greenhouse, and you proved to be a natural-born tour guide. "This is the rubber tree," you told the visiting ladies. "His name is Livingston, don't ask me why. And these are the orchids, and that is the hibiscus, and the name of that fern is Fluffy Duffy, and this is the Bird of Paradise only it has smut on its leaves. This is Boogie the bougainvillea, and the rest of the things are geraniums and stuff." Next year, Disney World.

Along in February came the great Girl Scout cookie sale. You won a book bag, a pencil box, and all that other junk— this is getting to be an old story—by selling 124 boxes, of which grandfather bought 22. This is what grandfathers are for. They have practically no other role in life.

It's great to see you so active in the Girl Scouts. You may remember this summer as the summer you went to Girl Scout camp and came home with a sunburned nose and 14 merit badges, including a badge for "aerospace," for heaven's sake. You also qualified for an "advanced beginner Red Cross certificate" in lifesaving. Nice work, my love.

Once I asked you to plan your perfect dinner. There was a considerable furrowing of the freckled brow. "Crab salad," you said finally. "Lasagna. One of those French pastry cream cakes for dessert. And a pitcher of milk." This is not how we keep the old weight down.

This summer, in between Girl Scout camp and 4-H camp, you're doing a lot of dreaming about the new house your mother and father will be building. You have your eye on the scrap lumber for a tree house, and your plans are taking shape dream by dream. This will be a hideaway to read in, where you can look at the Blue Ridge Mountains and see forever, and you won't let Douglas in—he can't climb up a knotted rope. From your tree house you can see the pond where the beaver is building his house. The supporting posts for this mansion will be set in concrete, but sigh, cement costs an awful lot of money. Honey, I tell you, that is the way homebuilding is.

In September comes the sixth grade, with a couple of favorite teachers for math and English and history and all that stuff, but September is a long way off. Meanwhile there are books to be read and trees to be climbed and animals to be watched, and of course, an eleventh birthday to be properly observed. Will you remember what you wanted for this birthday? A tackle box, a pair of skates, and something for the stamp collection. That's neat, Heather, and so are you.

Love,
Grandfather

AT TWELVE, JULY 28, 1982

Dear Heather:

Your letters from camp have been arriving in veritable torrents—to me, to your mother and father, to brother Douglas, to Cousin Alina—and we have passed them around. From these letters we gather that (1) you once got homesick and cried, (2) you are making a bracelet, (3) you are in a play, (4) you are taking some tennis lessons and (5) you are getting a tan. All this is to be expected, but if your camp is any decent sort of camp at all, you also are (6) scratching chigger bites and (7) peeling your sunburned nose.

In your spare time, if I am not mistaken, you are sitting on your cot in Bunk Four grousing about the food and hungering for mail. "Please, please, please," you said to Alina, "please write or I won't eat and I will die." To your father you voiced a threat even more ominous: "If you don't write I will elope with Alex." Your message to brother Douglas was direct and to the point: "If you don't write I will beat you up when I get home."

As for the camp food, you have now eloquently advised all of us that the food is horrid, dreadful, uneatable and, as you spelled it, "grose," which is close.

All this strikes me as par for the summer-camp course. All camp food is horrid (though some is more horrid than others), and no 12-year-old ever has been known to get enough letters. You will find this hard to believe, but your grandfather was once 12 years old, and he went to a YMCA summer camp in Oklahoma, and he complained of terrible food and no mail—and that was 50 years ago. Some things, among them summer camps, never change.

You asked me, "What's going on?" Let me see. The five baby wrens that were nesting in the hanging basket by the kitchen grew up and flew away. The baby swallows have done the same thing, and now they are putting on a flying circus by the red barn. We have a groundhog whose hole is not 50 feet from the house. He bustles up when he thinks no one is looking, and eats the birdfeed that has fallen from the feeder in the oak tree. Half a dozen quail have discovered the same free lunch.

Out in the garden the tomatoes are finally beginning to ripen. The zucchini is coming in, as it always does, in quantities sufficient to feed your entire camp for the rest of the summer. We are picking a dozen cucumbers every morning; they are turning into pickles by night. I think we have licked the rabbit problem, though the barbed-wire barricades and machine-gun emplacements strike some visitors as just a little odd.

What's going on? Here at home you haven't missed a thing. The summer days are like all summer days—hot and humid most of the time, but in the late afternoon the thunderheads roll up over Turkey Mountain all black and purple, and we run around closing windows. Then, crash, bang! It pours for 15 minutes. This doesn't help the fresh-cut hay, but it makes the zucchini grow.

Beyond the borders of Rappahannock County, a lot is going on. I have lost track of the wars and would rather not tell you about them anyhow. You have better things to think about on a 12th birthday than man's inhumanity to man. For the time being, let us talk about copper bracelets and clay pots and toasted marshmallows and how you hit a forehand and whether you have learned to keep your feet together in a jackknife dive. The wars can wait.

These are the long summer days of your life, my love, when homesick tears are afternoon showers. They don't last long, and they help you grow. Give our regards to all your friends, and especially to your bunkmate who got her lip caught in her braces. And come home soon. You said in one of your letters that you missed all of us, even Douglas. Well, vice versa. That's Latin for we miss you, too.

Love,
Grandfather

ABOUT THE AUTHOR . . .

JAMES JACKSON KILPATRICK became a professional writer at the age of six, when he sold a poem to *Child's Life* for 10 cents cash. The poem honored Lindbergh's flight to Paris. He has been fiddling around with words ever since as a reporter, editor, TV commentator, and author of seven books. He is the nation's most widely syndicated political columnist.

Mr. Kilpatrick divides his time between Washington, D.C., and his home near Scrabble in the Blue Ridge Mountains of Virginia. In the capital, he covers the Congress, the Supreme Court, the White House, and the political figures that come and go. After 42 years in the news business, he qualifies as a certified pundit. In this role he writes what he calls some "exceedingly stuffy stuff."

When he comes home from the national zoo, he puts aside the business of bah, humbug. At White Walnut Hill he writes of the things that really matter—of birds and animals and good friends, of earth and water, of falling leaves and falling snow. When he is not at his typewriter, he is vigorously engaged in the sedentary life. He is a supervisory gardener, which is to say, he leans on a hoe while his wife does all the work. In the swimming pool, he floats; on the tennis court he hits little but junk shots. He has never been known to jog. He collects stamps and flags; he putters around with orchids; he bangs a piano. Politically he stays busy as honorary national chairman of his party, the True Whig Party. Since 1961 he has been the Number One Pea, Pro Tem., of the Black-Eyed Pea Society of America.

Mr. Kilpatrick and his wife, sculptor Marie Pietri, have three sons, five grandchildren, and one shelty dog, name of Happy. The dog was named for the kind of life they lead.

. . . AND THE ILLUSTRATOR

JEFF MACNELLY, cartoonist for the *Chicago Tribune*, also creates the syndicated comic strip, "Shoe." He keeps an office in Chicago and his home in Jetersville, Virginia. Twice Mac-Nelly has won the Pulitzer Prize for cartoons and twice, the coveted Reuben awarded by the National Cartoonist Society.